I DREAMED FREEDOM

An
Abused Muslim Girl's
Journey to Find
Freedom

I DREAMED FREEDOM

An
Abused Muslim Girl's
Journey to Find
Freedom

ISIK ABLA

This book is available on Amazon.com & www.IDreamedFreedom.com or order@IDreamedFreedom.com

"You shall find the truth and the truth will set you free."

I DREAMED FREEDOM:
An Abused Muslim Girl's Journey to Find Freedom

"He forced me to the balcony and put a bread knife to my throat. The sharp edge of the knife was just barely piercing my neck, and I held my breath to prevent injury. All kinds of feelings were flooding my mind at that moment, my thoughts mixed with fear, anger, and hopelessness. I believed I was going to die. At that moment it was impossible to believe that **God** had better plans for my life."

Introduction

No eye has seen, no ear has heard, no mind has conceived
what God has prepared for those who love him
(1 Corinthians 2:9).

When I look back from time to time, I clearly see God's hand over my life, even I couldn't see it at the moment. I am sure this happens to many of us. We look back on those times we were in darkness, lost, those times it was impossible to see the light or to have hope because our dreams were so crushed. Our dreams were shattered by brutal trials. We were stuck in our prison cells.

Then suddenly! Something happens.

A touch, a breeze, or some other form of wind: God comes and changes everything with one touch.

> *He turns our mourning into joy.*
> *He turns our darkness into light.*
> *We know at that moment—we will never be the same again.*
> *He fulfills our dreams in an unexpected way.*
> *Only a Savior can do this;*
> *Only the True Living God can do it.*
> *Only God can set us free, and give us a new destiny.*
> (From the author's journal)

A prison does not have to be a four-walled room. We all have been prisoners of our circumstances. When we find the truth, the truth sets us free.

"Then you will know the truth, and the truth will set you free,"
(John 8:32).

"Why am I here on earth? What is my purpose?" Many people ask these questions. What is the truth? Is truth based on our own wisdom and intellect? Can the truth change from person to person? Does it change from culture to culture? Who determines and decides what the truth is: our own minds, our parents, our friends, the world? Who has the final word?

I asked these questions all my life. I wanted to find the real meaning of living, the real meaning of my existence. I wanted to live my life to the fullest. I wanted to find the truth. Truth sets us free.

I am compelled to tell you that you are not reading this book by accident. You didn't just buy this book by chance, nor did someone just happen to give it to you. I used to believe in chance, luck, numbers, and all kinds of superstition. Not anymore. I believe in divine appointments. I believe in destiny.

In fact, I believe we all have two destinies. Yes, you heard me correctly: two destinies. One destiny is that we live our lives in our own way, just like Frank Sinatra famously sang: "I did it my way." The other destiny is that we live our lives according to God's divine plan, which is perfectly designed for each one of us.

At this moment I must stop and explain that walking in God's divine plan doesn't mean living a perfect life. His plan includes a lot of tests and trials. Jesus said to His disciples, "In this world you will have trouble. But take heart! I have overcome the world" (John 16:33).

However, when we look at the complete picture of the life that we can live with Him, we see a complete masterpiece.

God's work is like one of Monet's paintings or Beethoven's concertos. Every brushstroke, every color, every note makes that piece of art a masterpiece. This is God's plan for your life and for my life: that we would be a masterpiece.

His perfect will for us is not a life of failure, even though we may fail; not a pit of darkness, even though we may experience darkness; not a wasteland, even though we may waste some time and effort. His perfect will for us is victory, success, light, joy, and peace in the midst of the storms.

I am not here to proclaim that I know all about life and death. I am not here to proclaim that I am someone or that I know something. Let's get this straight from the beginning: on my own, I am nobody, and I am satisfied to be nobody. But in God, I become someone and something much greater.

I knew that my life was a failure. I was a mess. I was imprisoned in my own circumstances. But the day I met my Maker, my whole life changed. And I want to share my journey to freedom with you.

No matter how terrible your situation may appear to you, how hopeless the news may sound on every channel you surf, how discouraging your circumstances may be, God can change it all with one touch.

When we are powerless and helpless in the natural, then the supernatural power of God can take over our lives. The moment that we acknowledge His power, all of our sins, weaknesses, and failures vanish from us.

This is a simple message, my friend—very simple. And it is absolutely true.

This book is the story of my life. It is the testimony of an abused

Muslim girl who had neither self-worth nor respect. I was a prisoner in my circumstances, but I was delivered and set free by finding the truth when I met my Maker.

This book is my testimony. It is written to proclaim God's existence and power. It is written to help others who have failed. It is written to help others who have been used and abused and feel like they have lost it all. It is written for the ones who haven't lost it all yet, but will do so for sure if they do not realize and acknowledge their need for God! Finally, this book is also written to encourage the believer with a simple message: "Do not take what you have in Christ for granted. Never!"

Parts of my story may be disturbing to you. I was asked to water down my testimony by the first editor I picked for this book. She said my plot was too alarming. So I picked another editor who would not compromise. I will not accept a watered-down testimony for the comfort of anyone. When Jesus Christ went to the cross, His appearance was not eye-pleasing. He did nothing to make His testimony nicer or more appealing.

Just as there were many who were appalled at him—his appearance was so disfigured beyond that of any man and his form marred beyond human likeness (Isaiah 52:14).

The Bible tells us some of the cruelest stories of mankind just as we are. God doesn't seek to please any person's comfort zone or natural likes. He cares more about our eternal destiny than our comfort. For that reason, He gives us the truth in all its nakedness.

Today, we must open our eyes to realize that there is a world full of people out there suffering and dying without knowing the truth that they are loved by God. They are loved unconditionally by their Maker.

And my friend, whatever your circumstances today, you are counted among those people: you too are loved by God.

This is the time when people must know that God is limitless. He is able to do far more than we can ever imagine. When we give Him full control over ourselves, He will do miraculous things in our lives—more than we can ever dream.

"For I know the plans I have for you," declares the Lord, "plans to prosper you and not to harm you, plans to give you hope and a future. Then you will call upon me and come and pray to me, and I will listen to you. You will seek me and find me when you seek me with all your heart. I will be found by you," declares the Lord (Jeremiah 29:11–14).

Chapter 1:

Family Secrets

I was a chubby girl with brown hair and green eyes. I was almost eleven pounds when I was born. People said I looked like a one-year-old ready to walk. My parents rejoiced that I was a big baby. In my family, big was always a good thing. My parents lived on the first floor of a three-story home. My maternal grandmother and great-grandmother, who was the authority on Islam for my family, were living on the second floor. My grandmother's aunt lived on the third floor. My father, Mehmet, was the only male in the house. He had to deal with all the practical concerns of the house, repair broken items, and carry everything including groceries. I often felt sorry for him.

My mother, Nur, was considered a good Muslim, although she never covered her head. (In Turkey, covering the head is optional for women.) She prayed and fasted during the month of Ramadan. I fasted with her from the age of seven. That fast was the only thing that my mother and I had in common—even our faith differed, as I was deep into Islam and she only fulfilled certain customs to make herself feel good. She was a very smart and gifted woman, and she was unhappy as a housewife all of her married life. It was torture for her to clean, cook, and do other chores around the house.

One day I saw my father looking at an old, dirty gray shirt lying on the floor. He stared at the shirt for a while, then called my mother and asked, "What is this on the floor?"

"Don't you see this is a shirt?" she answered.

"I can tell that. But which shirt is it?" His voice rose. "Is this the white shirt I just bought from Vakko?"

"Yes, that is the one!"

"Are you crazy? Do you know how much I paid for this shirt? What is it doing on the floor?"

"I am mopping the floor with it," my mother replied, truly clueless as to why this was such a problem.

"Mopping the floor with a brand-new shirt?" He was screaming now, but she didn't back down.

"Yes. So what? It was in the dirty-laundry box anyway. Until I do the laundry, I will clean the house with dirty clothes."

Then it turned into a shouting match as usual. Cursing, slamming the doors, and threatening.

I was used to seeing my new white sweaters quickly turned pink or gray and two sizes smaller than they were originally. Every time my mother washed our clothes, we had a new style of clothes to wear. Whatever went into the washing machine never came out the same again.

My dad had a lot of complaints about my mother's housework that started many fights between them. She was not at all trained for housework when she was young. She grew up with maids and never had to do anything around the house. Her mother and her uncles were so sure that for the rest of her life, she was going to have maids. Well, it didn't work like that. When my father asked to marry her, her family said, "This girl doesn't know any housework. She cannot cook or clean." My dad said, "I don't care. I don't want to marry her to cook or clean, but to be my beautiful porcelain statue." She went through the same thing with her cooking. Our kitchen almost burned down a few times.

I, and eventually my much-younger brother, learned to laugh at these accidents. Yet, they were not funny to my father. The food always turned out bad when cooked and therefore was wasted. There was a big fight after each episode. We got used to living this way. We often ate in restaurants or ordered food to eat at home. I thought my mother was hilarious when she was cooking or cleaning. My father's sense of humor did not agree with mine.

My mother accepted the fact that she couldn't do housework well, and she never tried to improve much. She did not work outside the home, convinced that she was not good enough for anything. My father's verbal abuse contributed to this situation—even today, he calls her an idiot every chance he gets. Today, I see my mother as a woman with no identity. When she comes to visit, we'll take her to a restaurant and she'll say, "I eat whatever you eat." She has no identity, no self-worth. This was true when I was a child, though I could not see it so clearly then. She stayed home with me, her mother, and her cats.

Cats were the love of her life. She spoiled them a great deal and fed them with beef, which made our neighbors very angry. When you live in a Third World country where many people cannot find bread, feeding pets with beef was very odd.

Her intense love for cats had its roots in my mother's childhood. Her father died in a war while my grandmother was pregnant with my mom. She grew up in the house of mourning without any love or kindness toward her. Once she said that days, weeks, or even a month would go by without any kind words or touch. She grew up crying herself to sleep. Her maid dressed her and took care of her physical needs. And that was all she got.

When my mother was about three years old, she got lost in her parents' house. They searched high and low but could not find her. Everybody panicked. Where could she be? They finally they found her under her bed, fast asleep while attempting to suck the mother cat's breast along with the kittens. Sometimes she ate from the same dish as the cats, and she slurped from the cats' dish as well. She was close to being a cat herself—they had been her closest friends all her life.

Mother often said she loved cats more than people. I often felt sad that I was not getting any of the hugs and kisses that her cats were receiving. I didn't understand the strong bond between her and her cats. I thought she loved them more than me. That was a lie, but I didn't know it, and I hated her cats with a hatred born of jealousy. The truth was, my mother didn't know how to love people since she had never received love from them. I do not recall a single hug or kiss from her in my childhood. This hurt me a great deal. My mother and I never were friends. Her life was focused on her animals and my grandmother. She often reasoned to her friends that I was a very private girl and she respected my privacy. This was a nonsense. Every time I heard her saying that I was private made me very mad. This was a huge lie. I was not private at all. I just couldn't open up to her easily because of her unexpected reactions and our lack of friendship. I was able to open up to strangers but not to her. She was emotionally instable and she was not able to respond to me in a way that a girl needed. She didn't know how to respond but react. My every need of trying to share my struggles ended up with her hysterical reactions. She couldn't speak but yelled and screamed most of the time to the point of insanity. Then she would justify her irrational behavior as a reaction of a passionate person. There were times I received hurtful words, and there were times I received only a long silent rejection. If I didn't say or do anything the way she wanted, she wouldn't talk to me for days. It was a complete torture. She had tremendous control over me. The guilt trips, manipulations, fear and condemnation were the foundation of our relationship which left deep scars in my soul. Not having a friendship with my mother became a huge void in my heart over the years. Later in my life, I have met many young girls through the ministry who were distant from their mothers and who were also labeled "private" by emotionally abusive and controlling mothers. Later on, I learned that abused people most of the time abuse people. Hurt people hurt people. I know the deep scars of this mind torture. It took me years and supernatural touch of God to be set free from an emotionally disturbed mother's demonic spell.

Nevertheless, I always admired my mother's beauty. It was a love and hate relationship. I always wanted to be around her. Yet, I was fearful of disappointing her. I was often trying to get her attention and affection. After all, she was the most beautiful woman on the face of the earth in my eyes. I felt like an ugly duckling next to her.

I was not the only one noticing her beauty. She got so much attention that it was not easy to walk down the street with her! She had very long, blonde hair, beautiful hazel eyes, and a great, petite figure. She always dressed modestly and beautifully. Heads would turn when we went to the marketplace or elsewhere. She was very conservative, decent, and faithful, and protecting our family name was her mission. She would die before bringing any shame to her family. I admired her for that too.

People and their opinions about us were what drove us, and we would do almost anything to please others or try to fit with their standards for approval. We paid great attention to other people's lives, to how they talked and dressed. Although my mother was considered a good Muslim, she often lied to be accepted and liked. I had never seen her at peace. I prayed and prayed to Allah to give her peace and rest.

More than anything in my life, I wanted to please people—to be there for them, meet their needs, and encourage them to go on. I lived my life for other people. I learned to like what they liked, eat what they ate, wear what they wore. I was a people pleaser. I often thought that if I could, I would be a father for my mother. She certainly didn't receive any support from my father. He did provide food on the table and a shelter over our heads, but emotionally, he tore us in pieces with his addictions to sex and women. This destroyed my mother day by day. My mother never had a father and she never really had a husband. I wanted to be what she needed me to be. I couldn't.

I lived for her approval. Yet, I myself needed a father as much as she did. Later on in life, I learned that there was a Perfect Father, who loved me unconditionally and who could meet all my needs. But it would be many years before I came to that understanding.

Chapter 2:

First Anger

I was about five years old when I first realized how much my father was hurting my mother and failing us as a family. He came home for a short while from work on a day when my mother, often weak and needy, was having a very difficult day. I don't remember how it happened, but my father had to take me out with him. His mood was completely opposite my mother's: he was extremely happy. He was dressed sharply and smelled very good, which was rare. I was happy to see him so cheerful—his good mood was unusual.

He drove us in front of a hospital and tried to look inside through the main entrance. He couldn't see what he was hoping for. Then he drove through the street and parked. He was so happy that he couldn't contain himself. This was exceptional!

Then, to my dismay, a very beautiful yet cheap and easy looking woman walked toward our car. My father got out as she came close. She came and hugged him. Then they kissed. My father opened his door and told me to get out of the car. I didn't want to. He ordered firmly. I got out. He introduced me to her. She bent and held my chin in her hand and said, "Oh, she is so cute!"

I just pulled my head back. I cannot find the words to describe the anger in my heart at that moment. Probably for the first time in my life, I remember my anger, hatred, and undeniable desire to scratch her face like a wild animal. I cannot describe that anger, but I remember how it felt even as I am writing right now. That day, I signed a silent contract in my heart that I was going to hate my father for the rest of my life. I hated him. I hated him and hated him.

My father walked with the woman to her car, which was parked a little further in the lot. Then I saw him carrying a suitcase. He put her suitcase into his car's trunk and told her that he was going to pick her up in a couple of hours. I don't know if a five-year-old can truly desire to die, but my pain can only be described as suicidal.

My father and I went home. In a short while, he left me and my mother to go on vacation with that tramp. I saw my mother destroyed beyond words in front of my eyes.

Mother became addicted to anti-depression pills and tranquilizers. She was like a vegetable, lying in bed emotionless or sobbing uncontrollably as she had nervous breakdowns. My smallest mistakes were magnified, and physical abuse took place during her breakdowns. Then she would come back to her senses and felt sorry. This torment continued for years.

I was seven years old when one day I saw in the newspaper or a magazine an article about pills. I saw a picture of pill bottles and recognized them from my mother's stock. The article said these pills were illegal and deadly. I was gripped by a terrible fear that my mother could die. I had to find a way to rescue her! *Think, think,* I told myself. I cried myself to sleep that night.

In the morning, I woke up with the same fear. I couldn't stop thinking of those poisonous pills. Then I looked for my mother. She was sleeping or passed out on the sofa in the living room. I went to the shelf where the pills were. First, I wanted to throw them away. But I knew that was not a good idea. I could be punished severely, and she would just go and buy some more. I opened up one of the bottles. (There were no childproof bottles in Turkey back then.) My heart was pounding so fast that I could hear it. I took one of the pills to investigate whether I could replace it with candy or something. But I didn't know any candy that shape and color: green and white. Then I squeezed the pill, and it fell into two pieces as the capsule opened up and a white powder came out.

I knew what I had to do. I emptied all the capsules. I did the same thing to all the other bottles. I cleaned up carefully and placed them exactly the way they were. Then I went to my room and waited. Mother woke up after a few hours. I ran to greet her, but she was not herself. She had a hangover. First thing, she went for her pills. I was there trying to look as cool as I could look.

For a few years, I emptied every single capsule in every bottle in the middle of the night. She also had bottle of a liquid that she would take by putting fifteen drops in a glass of water twice a day. I replaced that liquid with water. She was putting water into water. My father caught me doing it when I was twelve years old. He laughed and encouraged me to do it.

I did this until one day my mother panicked: she'd forgotten how many pills she had taken and thought she had overdosed. She told me she had to go to the emergency room, that she'd taken four, maybe five pills. At that moment I couldn't hide it anymore, and I started laughing. I told her that if she took the entire bottle nothing would ever happen, since the capsules were empty. She didn't believe me, but she ran to check if there was any possibility it was true. She opened up many capsules, in shock that all were empty. I told her she had been taking empty capsules at least for five years and daily putting fifteen drops of water into water.

I was able to protect my mother through my middle-of-the-night raids, but I couldn't help her heart. She was tormented because of my father's unfaithfulness. He never showed any remorse and justified his affairs as part of being a "real man." Even when I asked his permission to write down some of these events (there are many others that are not written), he happily told me he had nothing to be ashamed of.

Chapter 3

Oscar Night

Throughout the years, my parents' fights became more intense. We had everything but joy and peace in our home. Fighting, cursing, and slamming the doors became the everyday routine. My mother and father became put each other down daily with harsh words. There was no respect or love between them. My father's so-called "business travels" increased. If Mother wasn't yelling and screaming, there was silent grieving in our house.

As my mother found out about more and more affairs, my parents finally got divorced. She took me to the courtroom with her when the judge divorced them. I was so helpless. I had no power and control over any of these things, and my heart was broken into a thousand pieces. The beatings I received at home didn't hurt as much as my parents' harsh words. As a little girl, I believed the words that came from their mouths in moments of anger. I believed that I was not good enough for anything. I believed I was ugly and stupid.

When my parents fought and the abuse got intense, I used to go to my room, close the door, and hide under my blanket. My parents' harsh words would echo in my ears. I would cry for a while. My child's mind would repeat the words continuously as if I possessed them for myself. I would lift my blanket like a tent on my knees and dream.

There is nothing as precious as a child's dreams. They are so pure and unadulterated.

In those dark days of my childhood, I tried to dream something wonderful to ease my pain. I usually dreamed myself somewhere like the Oscars in Hollywood, California. I would be walking on a red carpet, wearing a beautiful white gown with ornaments of pearls and diamonds. Then my name was announced: "And the Oscar goes to Isık." I would go up to the platform to pick up my prize. All I cared about was that my parents would be proud of me. I wanted so badly to prove myself to them. I would take my prize and say, "This prize is for my mom and dad. Thank you, Mom. Thank you, Dad."

In my dreams, they were there and they were proud of me. I was not the abused and worthless girl to whom they often said, "You are stupid" or "You are not good for anything!" In my dreams, I was someone they were proud of.

But God's dream for my life was better than my own dreams. And though I was just a child, I was on my way to discovering a little about that dream.

Chapter 4:

Visitation from Jesus

When I was a little girl, there were times my body was covered with dark marks and bruises because of my mother's beatings. The same was true of my soul. Along with my desire to please people, I just wanted to be invisible. I believed there was nothing significant about me—I felt I was insignificant in every way to everyone. I was no good. I always caused trouble, and I was blamed for the misery of the family. I prayed and prayed to my god, but there was no answer.

At that time, all I knew about God was what I was taught in Islam. While my peers were playing with their toys, I would rather be praying to my god like the adults. I was very interested in talking to him. I memorized Suras—verses—from the Koran and recited them over and over. My great-grandmother, Nene, used to take me to a local mosque. I would cover my head and take my little Koran and follow her. After all, she had taught me everything I knew about Islam. I received her love and attention as long as I was a good student. When the abuse was intense at home, she was my hiding place.

But nothing could draw my attention more than the one whom, I believed, had created me. "He is my Maker. He has the answers I am looking for," I told myself. My faith was so strong that it was noticeable to others. As our family life became more dysfunctional, I turned closer to the one who had created me. I had the faith of a pure, childlike heart. Yet, I also had one big fear that was controlling my life: death. My faith had no power over this intensive, controlling fear, and it controlled me every hour. If I was in a car, I would fear that the car could crash anytime and I would die. If we were walking on the street, a car could crash into us, and we would die. Bad people could come and kill us. I remember once, I was looking at a mirror and my mother came into the room. She said, "Keep looking at the mirror. One day, the devil will appear from the mirror and will ask you "Are you looking for me?". And he will kill you. I couldn't look at mirrors for years. Another time my mother was so much in fear of me losing my virginity out of wedlock, she told me that intercourse was so scary as if a bread knife was cutting me through. She said I could even die of bleeding. That affected me for years as well. My fear was not based so much on how it would happen, but on death itself. Death was a terrible, deep, dark dungeon. In the middle of the night I would wake up and cry out, over and over again, "I don't want to die! I don't want to die!"

One night when I was five years old, I had a dream. A man was dressed all in white, and he was smiling at me. There was a brilliant light around him. I could think of nothing more comforting than his warm smile. I felt a peace I had never experienced before. I saw myself as a grown-up, standing in front of him. He came closer to me. It was overwhelming. I felt very small and powerless in front of His greatness. His presence was breathtaking.

He said, "I am Jesus. Isık, do not be afraid of dying. You are not going to die. You are going to have eternal life. But your mother will die." I knelt before Jesus crying, "Please, Lord, please do not make my mother die. Please."

He lifted me up, wiped my tears with his hands, and said, "Then you need to pray for her."

Then I woke up. I ran into my parents' bedroom and woke them up, saying, "Mommy, I don't want you to die. I don't want you to die."

My mother said, "Calm down, I am not going to die. Who said I am going to die?"

"Jesus," I answered.

Now I had my parents' attention! As soon as I uttered that one word, they were sitting up and looking to me for more information. I continued, "Jesus. I saw Jesus in my dream. And He said that I am not going to die. I am going to have eternal life. I am not afraid of death anymore." I started crying. "But he said, 'Your mother is going to die.' I begged him. And he said, 'Then pray for her.'"

My parents asked at the same time, "Who spoke to you about Jesus?"

It was like I had done or said something terrible. Fear that I had done something wrong and that I was in big trouble came upon me. Confused, I answered, "Nobody. I told you, He was in my dream." They did not believe me and wondered who had talked to me about Jesus. They both asked how it was that I could have a dream about Jesus if I knew nothing about Jesus. I couldn't answer their questions—all I knew was that my greatest fear was gone.

Death was never to bother me again. After that dream, I started to say, "I am not going to die," and people would laugh at me. Years have passed, and I still remember the comforting presence of Jesus in my dream. Somehow, that dream gave me hope for the future. It was hope I would sorely need, for before things got better in my life, they would take several turns for the worse.

Chapter 5:

A Dreamer

I have been a dreamer all my life. I like to think and dream. I loved to be in nature and dream about things. But perhaps the greatest influence on my dreaming was that of books.

I give my father the credit for teaching me passion for reading and learning. We both worshiped knowledge for many years. In high school or college, I read a book called *Faust,* written by Goethe, a famous German philosopher. Faust, the main character, sells his soul to the devil for knowledge, thinking that knowledge will give him power. My father and I at one point worshiped knowledge like Faust did. I think knowledge gave me the confidence that I was desperate for. It temporarily cured my insecurity. But it was only a temporary solution for my wounds.

I remember the days my father came home with boxes of books, including many world classics and children's books. He bought French, German, Italian, Greek, and Russian literature. In my imagination, I started living in the countries represented by the books I read. I loved the characters in these stories. Jules Verne was one of my favorites when I was in elementary school. I learned to dream through his books, such as *Twenty Thousand Leagues under the Sea* and *Around the World in Eighty Days.* Then came Edgar Allan Poe, Shakespeare, Hemingway, and others. New horizons opened before me. I had two lives. One was miserable, full of bitterness and pain. The other one was a life of dreams, freedom, and adventures. It was my secret life, and I loved it.

Since my father saw that I enjoyed books, he bought me more and more of them. When I finished the books he gave me, I would read the same ones again and again until he brought me new ones. I would memorize the most amazing passages from Shakespeare and make little plays in my room in front of the mirror. I was the main character and then the supporting characters. I was a knight and then the princess. I was King Henry and Othello. I would put my bedcovers like a shawl around my neck and say, "To be or not to be." I would stay in my room all weekend, reading and putting dramas together. I didn't care where we went for summer vacation—my books and dramas went everywhere with me, and so did my dreams. I would easily miss meals if my mother would let me.

These books opened a new horizon in my mind. I knew that someday I would be living in a different place, in a foreign land, loving different people and singing their songs. When I thought of that, my heart pounded faster.

This dream world was hidden in my heart. Then my father started a new line of work in his business: architectural designing for theaters and playhouses. As he saw my great interest in theater, he started taking me to the live theaters and playhouses. I saw some plays more than twenty times. I would crawl into a dark back corner of the theater and watch the books that I had read coming to life. It was breathtaking.

My father was constructing one theater house, of the biggest ones in the country, that was like the Carnegie Hall. I was there every day after school and my entire summer. I would help set up the stage and then watch the rehearsals over and over. I memorized everybody's parts. Those were the best days of my childhood.

Yet, there was somewhere deep inside hurting—hurting terribly. And I had no idea how to deal with it. I wanted to fix everything. I wanted to fix my mother's depression. I wanted to fix my father's unfaithfulness. I wanted to change the world around me. Yet, I felt so powerless to do anything, and the tornado in my heart was stirring.

As much as I hurt, I buried myself under my books. I read and cried for hours. I remember one of the books that affected me most: a French classic called *Les Miserables*. It was about a convict, Jean Valjean, who got caught stealing bread. The story took place just before the 1879 French Revolution. Valjean was a prisoner for nineteen years in one of the worst prisons in France. Then he escaped.

But his escape didn't go smoothly, because a police officer made it his life's mission to find him and return him to prison. I loved the part where Valjean has no place to seek refuge. All the inns turn him down because he has a criminal record. His last chance is at the bishop's house. Even today, just thinking about this part of the story makes my heart beat faster! He knocks on the bishop's door, and the bishop welcomes him as if he were not a criminal but a respected man. Jean Valjean's encounter with the bishop changes his life. He surrenders his life to Jesus and becomes a new man.

Reading the story as a child, I cried at the part where the bishop says, "Today I bought your soul from the devil and gave it to God." I cried and cried and cried. In my early teenage years, I watched the movie based on this book at least thirty times, and it impacted my life greatly.

I was not more than fourteen years old when I saw this little ray of light appearing in the midst of my dreary world. I didn't understand the concept of a soul being rescued from the devil and given to the

Lord, but I felt my heart becoming more tender. I cried deeply inside myself, knowing that my soul needed to be rescued. I adopted Jean Valjean's personality as an extension of myself.

Reading the Koran was engrained in my early life, but it did not bring the same hope that books like *Les Miserables* did. It seemed that my childhood god, Allah, was angry at me. There were a lot of other scary things in the Koran too. I kept reading, hoping to find a little peace and happiness. I kept searching for the good things about my god.

Nowadays, everybody has some opinion about Muslims. One thing that I can tell you about Muslims is that, deep inside them, they all seek God, known to them as Allah. They all want to understand and not abandon their faith. Yet they do not fully understand how much they are loved by God. They work all their lives to be loved by Allah, to win his approval and please him. But they do not know that God loves them unconditionally. My present Lord God loves Muslims. Oh, how Muslims need to know this fact! We all carry a deep need to be loved, no matter what our religion is. I pray for Muslims continuously day and night, that they all may know how deep and wide the Lord God's love is for them.

Chapter 6:

Old Man on Roof

Before I formed you in the womb I knew you, before you were born I set you apart (Jeremiah 1:5).

Istanbul, Turkey, where I was born, is one of the largest and most crowded cities in the world, with over fourteen million people living within its boundaries. It is the most popular city in Turkey, a place where people from other towns and villages migrate to find better jobs and, they hope, better lives. Since Sultan Fatih Mehmet captured the city of Constantinople from the Byzantine Empire in 1453, the Turks have been living there. Some archaeologists consider Istanbul an open museum. Everywhere you go, there is history: mosques, museums, and churches. Most old churches are museums or office buildings today. Some of the buildings are in a state of near destruction.

The Bosporus Strait divides Asia from Europe, with two bridges connecting the two continents. I was born on the European side of the strait, which was a big deal for my parents. Turkey has a very small amount of land on the European side, for which they like to be considered part of Europe. For many years, it has been a dilemma whether Turkey is a European or an Asian country. In visiting Turkey today, you will see a mix of European and Asian cultures. It is very hard to separate the two. We have foods similar to Greeks, Iranians, Russians, and Syrians. I grew up being accustomed to all of these foods. For example, cow's brain and cow's tongue were my favorites!

My father had a large office with a warehouse in one of the old churches that became an office building. He often took me to his work. The church was in the business district, where there were many buildings hundreds or thousands of years old that were rundown and dirty. This particular church was fascinating to me. Its paintings and frescoes were very much damaged, but even so, the artwork of the columns, walls, stairways, and marble floor was a masterpiece. Everything was gray and under dust. Every time I went there, I discovered something new. My father used to dig into the walls of this building, and he found some crosses and iron motifs hidden by Christians who were under persecution during the fifteen century. He was collecting them, hoping to sell them one day and make a fortune.

Going to my father's work was a great treat for me. I was familiar with all the other businesses around there and used to go door-to-door to visit his neighbors. My father helped others around him to grow and prosper in many ways, so I took advantage of eating the candies that were offered for my father's sake.

One day, I was all alone and bored in my father's office. I wanted to explore within the building, so I started wandering around. I saw a tiny stairway going to the roof in the back of the warehouse. I thought it would be cool if I just climbed up to feed the birds. I took a large loaf of bread and headed up. It was easier to open the little door at the top of the stairs than I'd thought.

I went outside and sat on the flat roof. While I was feeding the birds, I got up and walked a little further from the door at the top of the stairs. There was an old man praying nearby. His presence startled me.

I stayed a little distant from him so I would not bother him, sat down on the roof again, and started tearing the bread apart with my hands and throwing the pieces around me. The birds started coming quickly. While I was feeding them, I watched the man who was praying. He was kneeling down with his eyes closed. He was old and skinny. From his outfit, I judged that he was poor: his pants were dirty and had holes in them, and his sweater was knitted with different colors obviously made from leftover yarn. His face was pale.

When he finished praying, I asked myself, *Am I in trouble? Will he tell my father that I was here?* It was too late to run back out of sight. He started coming toward me, and the closer he came, the deeper his wrinkles appeared. I thought, *Oh boy, he is old.* He looked very tired. Then he looked at me—directly into my eyes. I thought again, *Am I really in trouble?*

Then he asked with a loud, strong voice that was totally unlike his frail appearance, "Hey kid, what are you doing here?"

"Nothing. Feeding the birds," I said, trembling.

He laughed. "Feeding the birds? Huh. You wasted the bread for fun."

That made me angry, and bold. "No, I did not. They were hungry."

His eyes darkened with anger. "You are too outspoken for a girl. That is not good, you know."

I did not say anything. I just wanted him to go away.

"How old are you?" he asked.

"Eight."

"Eight? You look older. You missed the prayer time. You should be praying instead of wasting your time with the birds. I bet you do not know how to pray. Your father is rich. He does not need to pray. Huh."

I said loud and firmly, "I know how to pray. I know my suras. I know them all."

"I told you," he said, "you are something. You speak too boldly for a girl. And lying is a sin. How could you know all the suras? What a lie. Allah will punish you for that."

"I am not a liar," I said. "I know all the suras by heart. My great-grandmother taught them to me." Before he said anything else, I started reciting the suras in Arabic. He looked amazed and stood there while I continued to recite.

Then he interrupted. "Hmm . . . it is quite impressive for a girl to know them at a young age. Do you love Allah?"

"Yes. I do," I said.

"How much do you love Allah?" he asked gently.

"I love him so much that I would die for him," I whispered.

"Then you shouldn't miss the prayer time, or you will never see Paradise. And you should cover your head, since you look older than your age." He spoke with respect in his voice, and I nodded. He added, "And do not talk too much. You talk too much for a girl, which is not good."

I nodded again.

He said "God's peace is upon you" in Arabic. And I responded in Arabic. Then he left.

My heart was beating so fast that I could hear it. I ran back to my father's office and pretended that the encounter had not happened. I went to bed praying to Allah to forgive me for talking too much and hoping that I would not see that man again. It was only one instance in a childhood full of guilt and condemnation—trying to love God, but knowing he could never be pleased with me.

Chapter 7:

War in Bloody Streets

The 1970s were very dark years in my country, years of civil war between the communists and the radical Islamic parties. The fractured political scene and poor economy led to mounting violence in the streets between ultranationalists, who were fanatic Muslims, and socialists.

In 1980, the Turkish military troops ended this violence—but not before it had done great damage. Brothers killed brothers. Families were divided. Our country was divided. There was no peace. Terror was everywhere. I grew up being very alert to the sounds of guns and bombs. There was devastating mourning from the parents who lost their children. I saw mothers in the middle of the street, hugging their children's dead bodies and weeping and asking their god, "Why? Why?"

I asked the same questions over and over again. Why were people being killed? Why were women being beaten up? Why was there so much violence? My heart was troubled. My prayers were not answered. I became more bitter and miserable. I experienced more abuse as I grew older, and I lost my self-worth.

May 1, 1979, was a beautiful spring day. I was nine years old. My mother insisted that I go shopping with her. We were carrying our shopping bags across the street when suddenly we ended up in the middle of a battlefield. Hundreds of people were running toward us from our left, and another group of hundreds were on our right, with guns, knives, swords, you name it. We were both frozen in the middle of the street. Suddenly, someone grabbed my mother and me and pulled us aside into a store. We waited there until the fighting was over, while brothers killed brothers; friends killed friends. I can still hear the gunshots, the bombs, and the screams on that day. I did not cry at all, but I was terrified by the screams of hatred. When everything was over, when the silence after the gunshots reached us, it was time to come out of our hiding place.

Mother ordered, "Close your eyes and do not look. Do you understand me? You do not look. Do what I say." I closed my eyes and followed her directions. One moment I felt that I had stepped on something. I opened my eyes. There was a young man lying on the ground, bleeding to death from his throat being cut. He was looking directly into my eyes. I still remember those eyes—that stare from a dying young man without any hope. Then I remember my mother screaming, "I told you do not look; oh, you stubborn child!"

Corrie Ten Boom says in her book *The Hiding Place,* "The only way to show love to this polluted world is dying on a cross." She also says, "If people can be taught to hate, they can be taught to love."

As a smaller child, I had been terrified of death. But today, May 1, 1979, when I saw death at nine years old, was the first time I really thought about life.

Chapter 8:

Teacher Strikes Girl

Being female, whether a small girl or grown woman, was considered a severe hardship in Middle Eastern culture. As a female, you were easily given a derogatory label. I was taught not to laugh loudly, not to speak loudly, and not to look a man in his eyes—not even to be caught looking in *anybody's* eyes. These acts were considered indecent. A woman who was caught looking in a man's eyes was considered sexually promiscuous.

I received a lot of physical abuse from my elementary school teachers. Especially there was one that would beat me up without mercy in front of the classroom. Her name was Ms. Gonul. I was around seven years old. I had a serious eating disorder. These were the miserable years of my life. I was rejected at home, rejected by friends, feeling unloved and unwanted. The only way I could get attention at home was by not eating. This was becoming a serious concern in the family. This was the only way I was feeling their love and attention by their worry for my life. My mother communicated her concern to my elementary school teacher. She bought gifts for her to pay special attention and care to make sure I was eating my meals at school. However, my teacher had carried her responsibility much further than accepted. The days that I didn't eat my meals, she would take me in front of the classroom, slap me, pull my hair, kick me and shout, "All of you look and see what happens to an idiot who doesn't eat her food. This is the stupidist girl in this school." You can imagine the bullies in the classroom watching the scene and being anxious to get their turn to beat me up during the break. When I came home and reported these incidents, my mother's response was "This is why you should eat your food. Don't blame anyone, but yourself." This was the comfort I received from my mother.

During my middle school years, one day the school administration combined my class with other classes in the library. The library was packed with students talking loudly, laughing, horsing and kidding around. It was mostly the boys who were rowdy—they had more freedom than we female students. The history teacher, who was my beloved literature teacher's husband, said, "Be quiet." None of the students seemed to respond to his command. Suddenly, he ran up to a girl and slapped her in the face so hard that the entire group of students became completely silent.

The poor girl was humiliated. She didn't say anything, but she looked the teacher in his eyes with hurt and bitterness. Her eyes were asking, "Why?"

He shouted, "You looked at me in my eyes, you whore!" Then he slapped her even harder in the face. All of us heard the hard slap as if it were a blow on our own faces. She continued looking at him in his eyes. In my heart, I begged her, *Please, stop looking at him in his eyes!* There was another slap. The teacher said, "You little slut! You unashamed, dirty creature, don't look at me in my eyes; I am telling you I will kill you." One slap after another was administered to the girl. Then she finally gave up.

I was crying silently. I swore to myself that I would hate him for the rest of my life. At the same time, that day I finally understood why my parents had warned me not to look a man in the eyes—why this was such a good quality in my mother's book. I was very conscious of her rule.

Years later when I came to America, I continued this Middle Eastern tradition. When I shared with a good American friend that I could not find a good job, she asked if she could interview me to help me work on my interview skills. In the middle of the mock interview, she stopped. "We do not need to go any further. The problem is obvious. You have not looked me in the eye from the beginning of this interview. Why?"

Confused, I answered, "I don't want to be disrespectful. I didn't want to give a bad impression."

"Why would you give me a bad impression if you look me in the eye?" she asked, obviously as confused as I was.

"This is what I was taught by my parents," I said.

She laughed and laughed. Then she said, "I am sorry. This is so silly. If you don't look at a man or even a woman in the eyes, you will not get a good job in this country. By not looking at the interviewer in the eyes, you are just telling him you are not confident that you can meet the requirements of the job for which you are interviewing. You show that you are not trustworthy, and that you may even be lying. You must look the interviewer in the eyes! Can you do that?"

"I will try," I said.

She laughed even more at my response, but her lesson had sunk in. Years after this simple teaching, I have looked back and appreciated my dear friend for this small rebuke that has made such a difference in my life and career! Yet, many women in other parts of the world are under oppression and condemned when they behave in a way opposite to the traditional slavery of their countries.

The importance of virginity was also underscored and engraved on my brain. I don't remember a single day when either my mother or my father didn't emphasize the importance of my virginity. It was my one mission in life to keep myself pure until I got married.

When I was a child, my father and I were coming home from grocery shopping. We saw a man kicking his daughter and spitting on her. She was on the ground in the mud, with her father screaming and yelling at her, "I am going to kill you! You are dead! You are finished!"

My father turned to me and said, "Never *ever* let this ever happen to you. You'd better die than lose your virginity."

Every day in the news, we heard that fathers were killing their daughters and brothers were killing their sisters because they had lost their virginity. It was called "honor killing." This is still practiced in many parts of the world: if the brother doesn't kill his sister who has lost her purity, then the father of that family is expected to kill both of them.

Where I grew up, it was culturally okay for a man to live in lust and sexual immorality. But if a woman became loose, she was despised, outcast, or penalized with death. I remember my mother taking me to a gynecologist when I was fifteen, sixteen, and seventeen years of age to see if I was still a virgin. She would take a deep breath every time I was examined by the doctor. Those visits were the only times I ever saw her smiling at me and saying, "Good girl." I felt like a gold medal winner in the Olympics, and all I did was keep myself pure.

Today, my perspective on all of this has changed. Even though virginity was overemphasized in my upbringing, I am thankful that I was raised with values of purity—it seems that these values are not practiced much anymore in the world! But my choice to remain pure was not really a choice: the only choice I had was to remain pure and holy before Allah. After all, I could have been killed if I didn't! This purity was not coming from my righteousness, but from an outside obligation. Yes, it was good to be holy. But true holiness starts in the heart. Holiness cannot be dictated. Holiness cannot come from external rules or regulations. Whatever I did as a good Muslim woman, I learned that I could not do enough for either man or my god, Allah.

I have learned since I became a Christian that even if I dress, behave, or speak conservatively, it does not make me holy on the inside—and that is what matters to the Lord. Only the True God can make us holy inside. An inside cleansing and purification done by the True God can bring a change of attitude in how we dress ourselves on the outside. We will want to dress more conservatively, not seductively, and to behave with true modesty and purity. Before I change my appearance on the outside, I first need the inside of me changed by the Lord God's supernatural power. For this to happen, I must have a personal relationship with Jesus Christ. Otherwise, His power cannot operate and do His marvelous things in me.

Without acknowledging the True God and receiving Him in my heart, I could not allow Him to start working in my heart and life. I have finally understood that without a personal relationship with the True God, I will only have a religion, tradition and rituals. This can make me feel good temporarily but not save my soul eternally. I prayed five times a day as a Muslim woman; I dressed as holy as I could, and I fasted. I thought I was pure in my heart. I believed that I was innocent in many ways, since my thoughts were not being defiled by men. (All I dreamed about men was that I would fall incredibly in love like in the story of Romeo and Juliet and get married and kiss!) But I did not have a relationship with God, and so my righteousness was never more than skin-deep.

All of this cultural background influenced the way I related to boys all through my childhood and teenage years. No boy I liked in high school liked me back. There was nothing about my appearance that was significant. Although I had some boys as friends, I was settled that they were only my friends. I was satisfied in my heart that I was not pretty. Boys told me that I was ugly. But never did they say that I was beautiful. So I eliminated from my mind any thought that any boy would be interested in me. I established good friendships with some boys, knowing that I was not interested in them and they were not interested in me.

Then a few of these boys opened up their hearts to me. I had a hard time believing that they had feelings for me—I thought they were setting me up so that other pranksters could come from behind the curtains to laugh at me. I never dared to have an interest for a boy until I graduated from high school at sixteen years of age. But our interest in each other was so innocent compared to the uncontrollable sex expressed today. I was looking for true love and care from the opposite gender, rather than physical intimacy. I believed wholeheartedly in the Romeo and Juliet kind of love. All my years of reading and dreaming had done their work. I sought that romantic and utopian love for the rest of my life.

Chapter 9:

Reading Faces

*With every sunrise we leave our childhood fairytale stories
behind us a little more. Actually, it is not the sunrise that pulls
us away from our dreams. It is the "sun" inside of us that rises
and disappears again and again each day. When we finally
find the truth we will be completely changed and transformed.*
(From the author's journal, 1983—Istanbul)

I was a loner as I grew up, a classic "weird kid." I was so shy that I would make every effort not to cough or sneeze in public so I would not attract anybody's attention. I used to put my hands on the cold metal legs of my desk in the classroom, then put my cold palms on my hot red cheeks to cool them down because I blushed so easily. I always had a hard time making friends.

I remember my first year in middle school. I was deeply lonely. I definitely was not the cool kid, and I never became one. I only had one girl friend. But I couldn't get together with her often. I assume my mother took pity on me, because although we never made a big deal of birthdays, this year she wanted to throw me a nice birthday party at home. I called all of my classmates and my friends in the neighborhood. I waited for hours in my new dress, along with my birthday cake with candles on it. Not a single person showed up. I was heartbroken.

When I was nine years old, I invented a game that only I could play by myself, which I called "watching people." Yes, that was my game:

watching people and reading their stories on their faces. I would look at them carefully, trying not to be noticed. And so I learned that people had stories written all over their faces. They were all going somewhere. They had thoughts, dreams, pains, loves, plans, even hatreds. During my youth, looking at people was the most interesting thing I could do. I used to look at people's faces so long that I would irritate them. I was often asked, "Hey kid, why are you staring at me, huh?"

But I couldn't stop doing it. I loved reading their wrinkles, tears, angers, hopes, and pains. When I was in high school, my math teacher and guidance counselor, Cicek—whom I loved—said, "Isık, the way that you look at me and others makes us uncomfortable. Why do you do this?"

"It is a game," I answered.

"A game?" she repeated. "What kind of a game is this?"

"Reading people's stories from their faces," I said.

She was confused. "What stories?"

"Their story, the purpose of their being and how they handle life."

A small smile crept onto her face as she listened. "How do you do that?"

I answered, "It is easy. Their stories are written all over their faces."

"What is my story that you read when you look at me?" she asked, obviously interested.

I hesitated. After all, she was my dearest teacher. But she encouraged me: "Tell me, I am curious."

"You look hurt," I finally said. "You think there is no way out of your situation." Before I finished reading her face, I saw tears in her eyes. She just gave me a big hug and left.

Shortly after that, I heard that Cicek was divorced. Divorce is one of the most terrible things that can happen to a woman in a Muslim country. My teacher had tried to fix her life and put everything in order by herself, but she had failed. She encouraged me to go to college to study philosophy, literature, or physiology. I took her advice and went into literature.

On my high school graduation day, she asked me, "What story do you read when you look at your own face?"

As soon as I got home, I looked at my face in the mirror and cried the rest of the day. There was no joy, no peace—only sadness, loneliness, disappointment, and hurt. I asked myself, "Who can help me change what I see here in the mirror? Can it ever change?" Again I looked and saw all the oppression that was taking place in my life. Much later, as a Christian, I looked back on those years and expressed some of the loneliness I felt in a poem:

> *While I was coming home*
> *From a distance*
> *No one told me*
> *You were there waiting*
> *With open arms*
>
> *While I was coming home*
> *From a distance*
> *I did not know*
> *You always loved me enough*
> *To die for me*
>
> *While I was coming home*
> *From a distance*

I did not know
You were calling my name
And praying for me

While I was coming to my Father's house
From a journey
With hurt and wounds
I did not know
You were wounded for my healing

Chapter 10:

Abdullah

Every year certain time, Muslims are obliged to sacrifice animals to Allah. This Islamic religious ceremony was depressing for me as a child, for I hated to see animals being killed in the streets.

Islamic life has always been a life of sacrifice. Islam has a long list of to-dos to get saved, yet even if you meet all the requirements, still you cannot know for sure if you will go to Paradise. Blood sacrificing is one of its many forms of worship. In Islam, blood sacrifices are made to please Allah. They are performed in order to attempt to get closer to Allah or to obtain his favor. Animals that are sacrificed include sheep, goats, cows, and camels. Wild animals cannot be used for a sacrifice in Islam. The religious ceremony of sacrifice may also be used for many occasions, including the birth of a child, the establishment of a new business, the completion of a construction project, or just to please Allah.

Every year in the Feast of Sacrifice, Muslims must sacrifice an animal according to their financial ability. If one person cannot afford an animal, two or more people can join together to buy an animal to sacrifice. After the animal is prepared to be eaten, the one who offers the sacrifice may eat a small portion of the meat. The rest of the meat must be saved for the poor and needy.

Every year, my family sacrificed a sheep to Allah. They would take a small amount of blood from the sheep and put it on my forehead for protection. Some years they would sacrifice a sheep to help an orphanage in the community.

It was usually my Nene (great grandmother) who performed this family ceremony. My great-grandmother seemed courageous to me to kill a sheep each year. When I was about nine years old, she decided that I had to be present to watch her kill the animal. She picked up a beautiful little lamb, and we went to the basement together. I was scared! But I knew that I must be a good Muslim since I was probably going to perform the same act someday when I was a little older. Therefore, I thought it was necessary for me to be trained on how to do it.

I decided to put my feelings aside and be strong during the killing of the little lamb. Yet my heart was pounding. I felt terribly mournful for the beautiful animal. My great-grandmother took the lamb and covered his eyes with a piece of linen. Then she held him between her legs with his head sticking out in order to stabilize him—and then she prayed and cut his head off from his body. Suddenly, there was blood everywhere, and the lamb's body was still shaking without his head. I don't remember anything else. I must have passed out. It took me months, even perhaps a year, before I recuperated from what I saw. Many times that horrific scene would replay in my memory, and I would cry many tears.

Years later, I traveled to a small town in the eastern part of Turkey during the Week of Sacrifice. I witnessed an entire town covered with blood from the enormous number of sacrifices. I saw a cow running down the street without its head. This terrifying scene, coupled with my memory of my great-grandmother's sacrifice, made me hate the Week of Sacrifice.

When I was eleven years old, my father brought a lamb to his construction site. His company was building a luxury office building. During their grand opening at the end of the month, he was going to kill this lamb as a sacrifice for the new building.

My father kept the lamb at his work. The building site had a beautiful landscape where the lamb appeared to be content. I would often go there to pet the little creature, and soon the lamb and I became friends. I tried to train him like a dog, spending hours with the lamb to teach him a few tricks. It was no use. The only things that we achieved together was that when I ran, the lamb ran after me. I had a lot of fun doing that. He would run after me so fast that when I stopped suddenly, he would crash into me headfirst. Sometimes I would fall into the grass from the impact, laughing and happy.

I named the lamb Abdullah. He would not come to me even when I called his new name—he was a stupid lamb, not that I've ever met any smart ones! But I loved Abdullah's company. I talked to him as my dearest friend. I opened my secrets to him, and he listened to me faithfully. We became very good friends. As the day of Abdullah's sacrifice drew closer, I became more depressed. This lamb was my only friend in the world.

I begged my father to save Abdullah's life. I cried for days and nights. When he went to the grand opening to sacrifice Abdullah, I stayed home, weeping uncontrollably in my bed. After a few hours passed, my father came back home. He told me that he hadn't sacrificed the lamb after all. "I just couldn't do it," he said. That day was one of the happiest days in my life.

Now I had a new pet named Abdullah, my dear friend. Those days with my little lamb are pleasant memories to me. True, our entire relationship was based upon my running across the field with him following me—but I had no complaints. I wouldn't trade him for the smartest dog.

A few months later, my father came home from his work with a downcast face and bad news. He told me that my dearest friend had wandered into the newly constructed building and fallen from the third floor, breaking his legs. Some wolves came from the woods and attacked him. Abdullah bled to death without anyone able to save his life.

I mourned for my lamb for a month. I missed him terribly. I became very lonely, since Abdullah was the only friend I had in this world.

Chapter 11:

My Most Important Decision

Although I was raised with only one brother, born fourteen years after me, my mother says that my brother and I make ten children in total. She had four miscarriages and four abortions between us. Her depression reached an almost incurable state. There was such darkness on her face and despair in her heart. At a young age, I was aware of all her struggles over each child, and they affected me deeply. I felt like an old lady inside even though I was in my elementary and middle school years.

When I was nine years old, my mother had a very big miscarriage. She was almost three months pregnant. I woke up early. My father was already gone. As I was getting ready for school, I heard my mother crying. I went to her bedroom. There was blood everywhere. She had a hopeless look on her face and was lying in the bed. I didn't know what to do. Was my mother dying? I started weeping and screaming, "Don't die, Mother, I love you! I will be a better child. Please do not die! I beg you stay with me!"

Barely able to talk, she whispered, "I called the ambulance two hours ago. It is late. I am losing the baby. And it is big. Help me—bring me some towels and a bucket." I rushed to bring towels, crying at the same time. For some reason, I could only think to blame myself. "I wish I was a better child. I wish I never made her so sad. Oh God, just let her live, please!

When I got back to the bedroom, I placed the towels between her legs. They turned red right away. Then the pieces of a little human body fell into the bucket. I was frozen, shaken from the deepest part of my existence. My mother was dying in front of me, and I was powerless again. There was nothing I could do. I was too small for this task.

Minutes later, one of Mother's friends came to our home. She and I went to the pharmacy to find something to stop the bleeding. All I could think was that my mother might be dead when we returned home. She was lying in bed, seemingly lifeless, covered with blood. I ran up to her, crying. She was breathing. The ambulance came while I was on the floor weeping hopelessly.

She survived. The doctor said it was a miracle for her to be alive after losing so much blood.

After seven days, my mother came home very weak. She looked very pale and almost disappointed that she had survived. There was more sadness in her eyes than had ever been there before. She was alive, yet she was dead inside. My grandmother, great-grandmother, and I took care of her to the best of our ability. She stayed in bed a long time.

No matter how sad she looked, I was happy that my mother was alive. I had missed her terribly. I helped take care of her, feeding and changing her, becoming her mother for a short while.

Most of the time, we live our lives as though we will never die. We hear that people are dying. We hear that people are having accidents and losing their loved ones. And all the while, dying sounds and feels far from us. Yet we are all destined to come to death.

As I reflect on that time, I am reminded again of the importance of certain decisions in our lives. When we are driving someplace and someone offers us a shortcut, we may take it or leave it. That advice may not have eternal value. It is a simple, insignificant decision. But if someone offers us the absolute truth, then we must evaluate it with all carefulness and seriousness. Because that absolute truth has an eternal value. It is significant.

Jesus offered us eternal life. He sacrificed His life for us so we will never truly experience death. He died in our place. He took our sins to His body.

My friend, this truth is more significant than any other truth you will ever face in your lifetime. The decision you make concerning it is the most important you could ever possibly make.

The most important question of your life is : "If you die today, right now or in the next few minutes, are you sure that you will go to heaven?" Will your faith save your soul?

As a child, I faced life and death many times. My mother's miscarriage. The dying young man with his throat cut. Even the lambs we sacrificed year after year. But it was years before I came to realize that life—eternal life—was a decision. Until then, I still had a hard road to walk.

Chapter 12:

My Brother: Bright Child

After so many pregnancies, doctor visits, miscarriages, and abortions, news of my mother's pregnancy brought joy to our home. I was fourteen years old, and I was going to be a sister for the first time. In the beginning, I didn't know how to feel about this new-baby thing. But soon, I found myself included in the planning, decorating, and shopping for the new baby, and I began to like the excitement.

Then at long last, a beautiful and healthy boy came into this world. My parents named him Can. I didn't quite realize that his gender was a reason for celebration. My father shouted to the rooftops, "It is a boy! It is a boy!" My mother was proud to have given birth to a son.

The significance of this really didn't sink in for me until the day my father bought my mother a beautiful Mercedes as a gift for giving birth to a boy. Many gold bracelets were given to her to put on her wrists, as was part of our heritage tradition. Also, my father hired a maid to take care of my new brother and my mother. I was forgotten as a member of the family, and I felt like "chopped liver" as Americans would have it!

I often heard my father spout off about what future plans he had for my brother. He would say to my mother, "You raised that girl, and look how she turned out. She is hardheaded. But I am going to raise my boy." Realizing how much my parents valued my brother over me took me a while, and it hurt me deeply.

No matter, I loved my brother. Can was beautiful. He had bluish-green eyes, beautiful white skin, and blond hair unlike most Turkish people. He was so special. I began to believe what my father said about him. Soon, I started worshiping my brother too, as if he was of a higher rank because of his gender.

Can turned out to have gifts that made him very special beyond his just being a male. Between three and four years of age, my brother was able to read and write. My parents took him to a child pedagogue who came from the US, scouting for genius children in other countries of the world. He represented an organization for super bright children. There were three-hundred-and-fifty-six super intelligent children chosen worldwide by this organization, and Can's IQ placed him in the top three. When we received his test results, we were all amazed by his answers to the most difficult questions at only four years old.

Can was placed in a very special school which was for only super bright kids to attend. He was also invited on to many TV programs for personal interviews. Even on TV, he would say incredible things to the hosts. They would not know how to hold a conversation with him.

My popularity in high school increased a great deal because of my brother. My classmates started visiting our house to meet him. On the other hand, I was called an "idiot" all my life. I believed this even more after Can's amazing success stories, no matter how much he was helping my popularity at school. He was the golden child, and I was the disappointment. Whether that was true or not, I believed it with all my heart.

My brother loved me. He loved me as if I were his mother, and I loved him just as much. He was so smart and adorable, and it was impossible to be jealous or angry toward him because he was very gifted. At least I had enough brains to figure that one out myself! Can was always by my side. He always wanted to spend time with me and my friends. He was very dependent on me in many ways. Even though he was the special one, he made me feel special all the time. He was tired of being treated like he was special. I was the only one who treated him like a friend.

There were many nights when he slept on my chest during his infancy. He enjoyed our tickling games and our kissing episodes very much. Over the years as we lived together in our parents' house, the fourteen years' difference between us disappeared. He was always there to listen and share things. He became a faithful friend and a humble servant when I needed him.

Chapter 13:

Unconditional Love

I passed the two most difficult tests in my life in order to go to college. Without a doubt, I knew what subject I wanted to major in: literature. I wanted to be a writer. I felt that I was going to change the world with my books. I even had a title for my first book, *The World that I Get to Know by Writing*. This title sounded incredibly profound to me. I dreamed and dreamed about my first book and even wrote a few chapters. I started sending my essays to many publishers, but I didn't receive any response for what seemed a long time.

During my freshman year in college, the editor of a school magazine contacted me for my essays. He seemed to be very interested in my writings, and he published some of them. Then one day, he wanted to talk to me about them. He met me on the college campus. Our conversation was short.

He said, "Isık, I have been an admirer of your writings, but they are all about unconditional love, and they do not make sense to other people. I enjoy reading them very much. But our readers are finding them too much like utopia. Also, your essays on death and hell are too depressing. What I am saying to you is difficult for me to put into words because I really like you as a person. But our magazine cannot publish your essays until you start writing on subjects that are more realistic and that everybody can understand. They don't understand unconditional love and stuff like that, even though I do."

I went home and cried for hours. I knew my writing career was over. Up until now, to be a writer was my biggest dream. Now, I had second thoughts. I wanted to quit writing altogether.

My second biggest interest was in evangelizing new candidates to become Islamists. With my Koran in my hand, I would go around the school campus visiting a group of atheists. They turned out to be very intelligent. Some students were very much into Marxism and Leninism. Then I learned a lot about communism to get prepared for debating. I liked to argue with them on the subject of God's existence. I would tell them, "Open anywhere in the Koran, and I will explain it to you."

They didn't know that my great-grandmother, Nene, had prepared me for these talks. She was fluent in Arabic and knew the Koran inside and out. I had always been interested in learning Islam. I thought if I learned about God and got closer to him, he would answer all my questions and help me in my misery. I was eleven years old when I started a Koran course and began to learn Arabic. It was summertime, and we were staying in our summer home. Other kids were going to play and swim. But I was gladly taking my Koran and covering my head and heading to the Koran course. At the end of the course, I became so radical that I wanted to dedicate my life to Islam. I wanted to cover my head all the time. My parents didn't like this idea—they were secular Muslims, and their appearance was modern. Covering heads was not very popular in their community.

These atheists were very impressed with my knowledge of the Koran. They would open up to the chapters dealing especially with allowing men to physically beat up women. I would say, "It doesn't mean every man can beat up his wife. It was only in the event of unfaithfulness, and it was not in a harsh way but to discipline them and save their souls from corruption." I felt like I could answer any of their questions. I knew they wanted to trick me, but I felt like I was prepared for the challenge. I would justify the most striking scriptures in the Koran. I would also use translation and interpretation differences to reason with them.

I felt as if I had answers for everything. And if I didn't, I could find the answer in a hurry. This atheist group had a leader who was an architecture student. This was his last year in college, and he was an atheist missionary as much as I was a missionary for Islam. He was not only a firm believer that God did not exist, but he also tried to evangelize with his beliefs. We despised each other. He and I would debate for hours in front of a crowd which became larger in size each time we met.

Our hatred for each other would show through our eyes.

He was extremely smart and educated. I remember studying the subject of communism until midnight in order to put him in his place. I studied every book that he'd quoted from the last debate we had together. This included many communist leaders who were his heroes. The books were written intelligently, and many of their ideas were very smart. It was not possible not to like the possibility of equality in the world. But communism did not work: it was collapsing from step one. When I researched communism, the first thing I found in the dictionary was "an utopia." Socialism, "a step to communism," meant a step to utopia. But the results of communism in the world were hardly utopian. Once I attacked the foundation, the rest fell apart in no time. The dream was good in itself. However, there was no evidence of its success in the real world.

One day after we finished one of our biggest debates, the rain started falling and the crowd began to disperse. I was picking up my papers, books, and Koran when he came over to me and started talking. He didn't appear to have hatred in his eyes anymore, but a weird, stupid look. He started quoting poetry at me. Then suddenly, he changed the subject and said he was in love with me. Nearly vomiting, I yelled at him, "I would prefer to die than marry an atheist! You are destined for hell!"

His rebuttal, "And you are not? How do you know that you are not going to hell? How do you know that you are going to Paradise? Is there any assurance in the Koran that you can show me?"

Even though he was an atheist, he had just asked me the most important religious question of my life.

He was right. I had no assurance of my soul's eternal safety. I went home crying silently on the public bus. I never showed up again to debate him. In fact, I never saw him again. But his question about going to hell remained in my heart, unanswered, for a long time.

Was there any assurance in my soul that I was safe from hell? I didn't even know the answer. I wanted to believe that I had won all the debates against him. Yet I knew for sure I had lost the last debate. I had no idea how to assert the eternal security of my soul, and this time, I didn't even know where to go to find the answer. Oh, how I hoped that someone could promise me some kind of assurance!

Chapter 14:

My Romeo and Juliet

I was sixteen years old when I started college. All of my classmates were a lot older than me, and I liked this arrangement. I met two new students who became good friends of mine. They both spoiled me as if I was their little sister. The classes were on literature, which made the courses extremely easy—I had read most of the required books already. When the teachers provided the list of the books that needed to be read, I didn't even have to write the titles down.

But reading wasn't our only chore. We had to learn six to seven dead languages along with Ottoman Arabic and Farsi, and not only learn them, but be able to read their literature and analyze their culture along with their authors. This task was not easy. Some of our teachers were secular, while others were strong in their faith toward Islam. Most of the required reading was Islamic literature. The poems and stories were very depressing.

One of the authors we had to learn from was Mevlana C. Rumi Sufi, a philosopher of Islam. He mostly wrote on love and acceptance of people, which was not the main theme of the Koran, but Sufi's theology was a new dream-order religion in itself. It is the closest Islamic denomination to Christianity. I compared the Bible with Sufi's writings and found incredible similarities. Yet, I felt that Sufi's teachings did not display the ultimate love that Jesus had for mankind, and I saw Sufi as humanistic. I liked his writings, but I didn't want to be a believer of his since he didn't completely acknowledge the Koran.

I thought I was a good student until I met a Muslim man in my college cafeteria. He was very knowledgeable about almost everything, plus, he came from a very religious Islamic family. His parents went to Mecca to do their duties to become a Hajji.

At first, we became good friends. We had a lot in common and enjoyed each other's company. Soon, I knew he was the one for me. We got engaged just after I graduated from college. I was nineteen years old. My parents were totally against our engagement. They fought with me over my decision to marry my future husband, and I fought back. My father even beat me up after I cursed him in order to defend my love. But all I wanted to do was to escape the misery of living with my parents.

After many struggles and tears, we got married that same year. But our problems began almost immediately: during the entire honeymoon, he didn't touch me. I was scared of sexual intercourse, and he seemed not to have any desire to touch me. Later on he tried. But each of his attempts were unsuccessful. I had fear and he had a serious problem.

Then the nightmare abuse started. During our engagement, he had shown some signs of aggressiveness. But it was nothing close to what started to take place after three months of our marriage. Just before this, I kindly spoke to him about my need to be touched. He blew up and said I was the one who had the problem, not him. Shortly after that, I dressed nicely and tried to look as beautiful as I could. I prepared a nice meal and lit candles. We were living on the sixth floor of an apartment building. He rang the doorbell at the first-floor entrance and shouted up to me to meet him downstairs so we could go to his cousin's house to eat. Well, I didn't submit to him—I wanted him to come upstairs to see my surprise. He kept ringing the doorbell. Then I opened the window and yelled down to him to come upstairs. I was so sure that he would be delighted to see me in my beautiful dress.

But as soon as I opened the door to him, he slapped me, kicked me, called me all the names a woman can be called, and cursed me continuously. My whole world was turned upside-down that night. From that moment on, darkness and despair grew more and more each day.

Several times I went by myself, without his knowledge, to a clinic or a hospital because I was bleeding so much from his beatings. Once I went to a police station and asked for help. The officer said, "Look at these buildings, houses, and apartments. They are all going through the same thing. We cannot take every woman in and arrest their husbands. Go to your home and behave better so your husband will not hit you as much. But if you leave him, you will become a whore or a prostitute. Don't disgrace yourself by sharing your personal stuff with anybody. Go home." I went back home and took his advice.

Abuse became a routine in my life. I got used to going to family dinners right after being beaten up. I learned to clean up and put makeup on my face to cover up my bruises. I learned to put on a turtleneck blouse to cover up my husband's handprints on my throat. I had a different cover-up plan for each situation. I learned to fake a smile and cry inside silently.

I remember one day when we were going to visit my husband's sister. We had gone to a grocery store to buy some bread. While we were walking to his sister's house, he started to hit me with the bread. My chin started to bleed, and he began slapping me in the middle of the street. In the beginning I didn't understand why he was doing this to me. Then I realized that he had been offended when I spoke to a boy at the register in the grocery store. My husband had conjured up evil thoughts in his mind about my conversation with the boy in the store. At that moment, he lost it. He left my face black and blue with bruises. Before we went inside his sister's house, we waited outside to cool down. I cleaned my face and put on new makeup. Then he held my hand as if nothing had happened. All that evening in front of the other relatives, he showed love toward me.

Years later, I found out that his punches and kicks left a permanent damage on my chin. As of today, it hurts me to speak for a long time. By the time my condition got better. Yet, I still prefer to write than to speak to communicate.

No one knew about my situation. My family, my friends, my coworkers—no one thought we had any problem in our marriage. We played "happy couple" to the best of our ability. My husband would kiss me and hug me publicly in front of our relatives and friends. I was deeply ashamed of the fact that I was married and yet still a virgin after several years. He blamed me and told me that I was a handicap.

A couple of years after our marriage, I read a magazine article about women being married and still being virgins even over ten years of marriage. I called the hospital number that was given at the end of the article. The woman who took the call was very gentle. She told me that I had to go with my husband for counseling. Softly, and with great understanding, she said, "The problem is not only on your side, but also your husband's. You are afraid that he will harm you. Is he physically abusive?" I didn't answer her. She repeated that we had to go as a couple. When he came home, I showed him the article and asked him to go to counseling with me. He said, "You are the one with the problem. Why should I go there?" That was the end of it.

Meanwhile, I continued to play along with my husband. I didn't want anybody to know about our predicament.

I had indescribable anger in my heart. I was bottling up everything. I would release my anger most of the time on the road. I had a serious road rage. I was a very skillful driver. More than skillful, you can call it crazy. If I decided not to give way to another car, this meant I was not going to give way. Many times, I scratched the side of my car and drove through the sidewalks just not to lose the race to someone. You think you just can see these things in the action movies. But it was a reality for my life. I could race with anyone to a point of death. I wouldn't care. I remember once someone was parked in my parking space in the neighborhood. I gave his car a flat tire. It came to a point that I was against the world and the world was against me. You can replace the "world" with "God".

Chapter 15:

Job for Escape

All my life, I had battled anger, sorrow and sadness. Now, I was experiencing severe depression without knowing it. I hated myself. I hated my hopelessness. I cut myself several times and even tried to see if I was capable of taking my life. In looking back, I can see that God protected me from killing myself, since He had better plans for me.

In the Middle East, many people go through depression without knowing it. It will slip up on you without you realizing it is depression, and it will take over anyone, no matter what age or gender. I knew of a child who was about eleven years old who was going through an intense depression. Many people are not educated well enough to recognize that they are in depression, and if they do recognize it, they are in a big dilemma: who are they going to see for help? Professional help for depression is not available as much in Turkey as it is in America or Europe. If you are seeing a counselor or any other professional help and someone in your neighborhood learns about it, you are labeled as a crazy person for the rest of your life.

At the time I was writing this book, I was in my thirties, and I realized that as far back as I can remember—over thirty years—my mother has been in depression. When I talked to her recently, she admitted that she has been going through depression for over fifty-five years. And she is not the only one. There are many women in Turkey like her.

Again, the question is, who can you go to for help? In Turkey, I had to wear a happy mask and cover up my failures and hurts. All of the dark side of life had to be hidden under the carpet. But those hurts were there.

Later on I have learned that the only thing that can heal you from depression is the supernatural power of God. When the laws of nature cannot operate and heal, then the supernatural power of God comes and does His marvelous work.

I had gone through intense depression since I was a little girl, not knowing what it was. As I grew up to be a young adult, I became suicidal. I prayed to Allah to take my life, because I felt I was too weak to commit suicide. In the Islamic faith, if anyone commits suicide, his or her soul goes straight to hell. I felt that I was already living in hell. But I didn't want to live there forever.

My life was confused and hurting. I hated my sadistic husband, and then at other times I loved him. I believed that I couldn't exist without him. I felt that he was my god. On the other hand, he was my best friend. He was my reason to exist. No matter how abnormal this existence sounds to me now, at the time I was totally blind, and I wanted to serve him with full submission and devotion.

When we got married, our friends started getting married and having babies. I felt very depressed because I had not conceived, and our abnormal lack of a sexual life left me feeling disabled. Yet, after the first year, I was thankful that we didn't have a child.

Anytime I tried to look beautiful, he would respond by saying, "Let's get one thing straight: you are not beautiful. Whatever you do, you are not beautiful. Don't you get it?" The only thing I could do was to believe him.

"I married you for your father's money," he admitted one day. He spent a lot of his free time hanging out with his fanatic Muslim brother. He also had drinking and gambling buddies. He spent most his nights in the casinos wasting our money. He could hardly keep a job for a month or two. He defended himself with excuses: situations at work would happen to make one of his peers jealous of him, and then his boss would fire him. But the excuses quickly grew hollow.

For me, work was a different story. I was fully trained by my father over the years to be a great employee. He taught me how to be a problem solver, taking initiative and being creative, and important principles such as attendance and attitude. In addition, for several years right after college I worked for a Japanese corporation. My superiors were Japanese. They were very hardworking, disciplined, and smart people. That was my first full-time job. I learned a lot from working with them: work ethic, dedication, organizational skills, and managing resources. My bosses always asked me which school I'd gone to and done my post studies at, curious as to where I could possibly have learned to work like I did. I never hesitated to tell them about my father's training and then my first experience of working for Japanese.

Going to work was the one delight in my life. Working was my biggest excitement and escape. I climbed the career ladder in small steps. I worked as assistant to the chairman of the board or president of well-known corporations, organizing events for high-ranked diplomats and businessmen and women in America and Europe. My husband had no problem with my success in the workforce as long as my paycheck ended up in his pocket. If I needed to buy shoes, he told me to ask my parents for the money. No matter how well I thought I was doing in my career, I had a great deal of fear that he would leave me. As much as he abused me mentally and physically, I could only find fault with myself. I believed that I was a bad wife and not good enough for him. I condemned myself and believed my own condemnation, and I felt like I deserved to be beaten.

Chapter 16:

Abuse During Ramadan

During the year of 1991, I was observing Ramadan—the ninth month of the Islamic year, which is kept by fasting all day long. I had honored this religious month every year since I was seven years old. During one of these days, I was beaten up by my husband at home. He knocked me to the floor and kicked me uncontrollably. This time, the abuse was sparked by my desire to continue working on my master's degree. We didn't have to pay for the extra expense—my parents had agreed to pay for it. Nevertheless, my husband screamed, "Studying is for stupid people like you!" He threw my books across the room, making a mess of the apartment. He hit me relentlessly until he had no strength left in him. I was on the floor, bleeding, and I begged him not to hit me anymore. I had very little energy to fight back because I had not eaten all day due to my fasting. I was shaking uncontrollably on the floor. All of my bones were hurting. My heart was hurting. I felt that I was not worth anything to anybody.

After another day of fasting, my husband told me to go to the mosque to learn to be a better person. I covered my head, and I went to the mosque. The building was crowded. When I sat on the floor in the women's section, they started to look me over. I was a young, nineteen-year-old woman at the time, and these women were eyeing me with hatred.

One woman said, "You are wearing nail polish. You must wash off your polish before the mosque prayer is read, or your prayers will not be accepted by Allah." I didn't respond to her statement. I hadn't eaten all day. Also, I had been beaten up most of the day, only up to fifteen minutes ago. I had no strength to answer her.

My silence made her even more furious. She told the friend who was next to her, "She will go to hell; she doesn't know. Allah doesn't like a prideful woman. This girl doesn't even answer me."

I remained silent. My body was aching so much from my husband's beatings. My heart was also aching from no one loving me but only rejecting me.

The imam started preaching, cursing the enemies, who were Christians and Jews. He was preaching a holy war, a *Jihad*. I just sat there and listened to his anger. He was saying "Amen" after each of his curses, along with the other participants. For a moment, I looked around, observing that there was no love being expressed here by anyone. There was only hatred.

At home, I had a violent man as my husband, and he physically abused me. At the mosque, the center of my religion, there was only hatred and terror. Where could I ever find peace and happiness?

As I sat on the floor of that local mosque dreaming of freedom, I didn't realize that I would be experiencing the peace I longed for very soon.

Chapter 17:

Plans to Escape

Four years into our marriage, we still hadn't become husband and wife sexually, and I was still a virgin. I was working in one of the most famous and successful textile and construction holdings in the country, which had twenty-nine other companies under it, as the executive assistant to the president, company owner, and chairman of the board. Every day, I went to work at 6:00 a.m.—not because someone asked me to go in that early, but because I wanted to leave my husband in bed, sleeping.

One morning, my boss came back early from his European trip and went directly to work. When he found me working in the office so early in the morning, he couldn't believe his eyes.

"What are you doing?" he asked.

"I am working," I said, as if it was a normal thing to do at that hour.

"Working this early? This is *too* early!" he exclaimed.

"I love my job," I replied.

As far as my boss was concerned, that was the right answer. He was a workaholic, and he liked being known for it. After he discovered me there that morning, he started giving me very important assignments. Soon after that, I was running part of his business, handling incredibly challenging assignments which included preparing events in Europe, especially in Germany. My husband didn't mind me traveling alone as long as I brought back his favorite apparel for him, expensive clothes from men's fine-dress shops like Armani, Gucci, and Versace. He would receive a new wardrobe every time I went to Europe. But as I traveled,

I started to see a different world. I was accomplishing important assignments and receiving a lot of praise from my boss—and from his peers. I was meeting important businesspeople, and whenever I had a little free time, I was out shopping for my husband.

Meantime, during these trips, I saw men treating women differently than in my culture. Women were more respected and valued. This was an eye-opener for me. Once, I was at a very important banquet with many diplomats and European politicians. I had to leave the dinner table to go to the lady's room. I stood up and said, "Excuse me." Then all the men stood up. I didn't understand why, and I asked, "Are you all going to the restroom too?" Everyone laughed. When I came back to the table, all the men stood up again.

Little by little, I started to see a new world where women had the same rights and worth as men. I started dreaming of that kind of life for myself. Eventually I started falling out of love in my marriage. Bit by bit, my thick head started getting the message that there was a better life out there for me. I started to dream that I was living somewhere else, enjoying a freedom I had never experienced before. I used to dream at the business meetings, in the airplane, and on the road of a little room or studio of my own where I could live without being treated like trash. I started embracing a life without a man who was constantly beating me up.

When I returned home from my business trips, my husband waited for me eagerly. First he would open my suitcases and check out the expensive outfits I had brought back with me. But no matter how much I bought for him, it was not enough. He often complained, "I told you ice blue. Does this look like an ice blue to you?"

With a lot of bribing and promising him a better life with more money, I was finally able to convince him to let me do my post studies in business. After so many times of being abused and tortured over my desire to study, I got him to agree to allow me to enroll in a night program. He was hardly ever at home anyway—he was either at the bars or the casinos. I would come home from classes to an empty apartment.

While I studied my courses, I continued to work in the business world. My boss agreed to let me limit my business trips to coordinate with my classes, and my husband and I didn't see each other very often. However, he was pleased to receive the financial blessings from my hard work.

As I studied and traveled, my expectations for my future became more encouraging. I realized I had never loved or been loved by someone special whom I could trust in a normal, non-abusive relationship. Even though we didn't see each other a lot, I was always under my husband's authority, and he had incredible power over me. I feared him greatly, knowing how capable he was of injuring me seriously or even taking my life in a moment of rage. Yet, despite my fears, I was slowly preparing myself and my heart to live without my husband. It was the bravest decision I had ever made.

Chapter 18:

One-Way Ticket to Freedom

I finally made up my mind to escape to freedom one day in 1994. That day, for no reason, we were both home together. Out of nowhere, he started blaming me for things I hadn't done. I watched in fear as he worked himself into a crazy mood swing. I kept quiet as he started threatening me with all the horrible things he would do to me if I left him. Then he started beating me up. Apparently, he was sensing that I was going to leave him permanently. He must have seen my decreasing love and interest in my eyes. He forced me to the balcony and put a bread knife to my throat. The sharp edge of the knife was just barely piercing my neck, and I held my breath to prevent injury. All kinds of feelings were flooding my mind at that moment, my thoughts mixed with fear, anger, and hopelessness.

Many times since, I have wished that I had been strong enough to take the knife away from him and use it to defend myself so he would have to beg for his life like I was begging him for mine. But I knew that I was not strong enough to break his hold on me. Then suddenly, he let go and ran out of the apartment. He must have gone to gamble and drink whiskey.

I knew that my escape from him was not going to be easy. He was financially dependent on me, and he had free range to abuse me. I had been dreaming that I would go far away—so far away that he couldn't ever find me. I dreamed of going to another land—to America, the land of the free. I had no idea how I was going to accomplish this task, but even dreaming about it gave me some happiness.

After I made up my mind to go, things began to fall into place. On one of my business trips to Paris, I met a Spanish girl, Maria. We became good friends. On one of her business trips to Europe, she came to Turkey in connection with the company where I worked. At that time, I showed her around the city, and our relationship became closer. I shared my dream of leaving my husband, and Maria encouraged me by giving me her phone number and address.

I knew that one of my problems was going to be attaining a visa. I called the employee in our company who was in charge of taking care of visas. My company had just opened a division in America. I told this employee very firmly that soon, I would be flying away for business. I didn't want him to obtain a visa for me at the last moment. Because of my high position in the company, he didn't even question me. He took my passport and within three days, brought back a visa with a ten-year extension. I couldn't believe what I saw! In that moment, I could *smell* freedom. Then I bought a one-way ticket to the US six months ahead of my planned departure date.

My husband's abuse had become even more intense, but now I had hope. I had a dream of escape, of freedom. There was only one thing left to accomplish—I had to obtain a divorce from my husband. I didn't want to leave with any connection to him still in place. But it was a known fact that a divorce in Turkey would take years to obtain, with many appearances in court. I couldn't afford to take that much time.

One day, I secretly met with a friend who had recently graduated law school, but who had never represented a case in court. She was shocked to hear of my predicament. She could hardly imagine the things I was going through.

While we were thinking of a way to get me out of my marriage, I mentioned that my husband had never consummated our marriage. To my surprise, she started to laugh hysterically. At first I didn't understand why she was laughing—all I saw was an overwhelming challenge. I was in a cage with no way out! But she kept laughing and getting on my nerves. Finally, when she saw the seriousness on my face, she controlled herself and she said, "I see a way out of your marriage. The law says that if a husband and wife do not unite in the first three months of their marriage, the court will automatically divorce them. We just need a doctor's report in your favor." Rather than the years I had expected, this could solve my problem within weeks!

But there was one major problem with this plan: since this fact was a disgrace to my husband's manhood, he would surely kill me for revealing it. For a man to be divorced from his wife in this manner, especially in a Middle Eastern country, is the greatest insult there is. We realized that we had to plan things out carefully. We left promising each other that we would think about how to accomplish the task.

A few days later when I came back from night school, I found my husband in the living room waiting for me. He appeared to be very angry. I decided not to take off my shoes but turn around in my tracks, telling him I had left something in the car. Then I ran out of our apartment as fast as I could. I got in my car and sped off. He tried to chase me on foot, but of course, he never caught me. He didn't drive or even own a car. He depended on his transportation from his friends.

I ended up going to my parents' house. My father opened the front door. When he saw me in the middle of the night, he knew something was wrong. He embraced me tenderly for a long time, unexpectedly showing me that he cared for me. I broke down and started sobbing, and I told him everything about my unsuccessful marriage. He had never known I was living under such intense abuse, and I watched his face darken with anger as I spoke. He was furious at how I had been treated by my husband. He assured me that my husband would not touch me again.

That night was the beginning of my life's change. From that moment, I went everywhere with an escort from my family. Meanwhile, I graduated from my post studies. My whole family was there for my graduation.

A couple of days later, with my father next to me for support, I called my husband on the phone and asked him for a divorce. Of course, he went berserk. I told him that if he didn't divorce me, I would go to court with a virginity report from the doctor and would send copies of the report to his family and friends. He began to curse me and make up all kinds of threats to try to scare me. Then he hung up on me.

For several weeks, he kept calling me by phone and threatening me. But he appeared to be more mellow each time he called. He knew, of course, that my father had learned about his abusive behaviors toward me. My father had a lot of his business people working for him as backup for my personal protection. He also had powerful friends in the community. Even so, I was mildly surprised when my husband's anger started to cool down, and he even started begging me to come back home—he was financially broke.

Finally, he agreed to a divorce if I would leave him some property we had jointly owned and also all the money in our savings account. I accepted the offer, with the modification that I would only give him half of the money. I also promised him that we would work on our relationship by starting our marriage all over again. That last promise was a lie, but he accepted all of the terms.

I was in shock that getting rid of him could be so easy. Years later, I realized that my fierce husband had turned out to be a coward. I also learned that when a victim will start to raise her voice and seek help by standing up for her rights, she is on her way to freedom. In my case, my violent husband became like a sheep, afraid of my father's wrath.

We went to court with our lawyers and witnesses. Even a journalist was present. My husband was in tears. I tried to look very strong and not yield to any of his games. I knew that I was in safe territory. Finally, the judge divorced us based on our mutual agreement.

Obtaining my divorce was easier than I could ever have imagined. After the divorce was settled, my former husband began to be very nice to me. He asked me to start our marriage all over again, as I had promised—falsely—to do. Since I had been his financial security, he spoke well of me in hopes of winning me back. He asked, "After all these years, how could you leave me just like I am nothing?" But I answered calmly, "All these years when you were abusing me, brutally beating me up, I was swearing to myself each time to leave you just like I have now!" His victim act was not going to work.

Several newspapers wrote about our divorce. A few days after my last encounter with my ex-husband, I was on a plane, flying to the country of my dreams. I was flying to freedom. At least, so I thought.

I never saw him again.

Chapter 19:

After a long flight, I finally arrived in my new home: America. When the plane landed, I wanted to shout with joy. I was twenty-four years old, but I felt eighty on the inside. I got through customs easily, reveling in the freedom and hope America promised. Later I learned that customs wouldn't allow anybody to enter the country with a one-way ticket and a tourist visa, but when I went through customs, nobody asked to inspect my airline ticket to see if it was one-way.

A whole new day had begun for me—but life was far from perfect. I began to realize that it doesn't matter where you are located in the world, you are still yourself. You have not changed on your inside because of your location. No matter how many countries you move to, or how many hairstyles you try, you are the still the same on the inside, in your heart. You can change your name, your nationality, and many things about yourself externally, but unless your attitude, your inner self, the inner being, the inner man or woman changes, you bring yourself and your circumstances with you wherever you go.

In my case, I carried my scars, my failures, and my victim mentality from my old country. I was all alone with myself for a few weeks until I could not bear being alone anymore. I didn't know how to survive without a man. This was ironic after all the physical abuse I had experienced from my first husband! But even though I was the one providing financially in my first marriage, I still needed a man to tell me what to do with my life. I was needy and terribly codependent.

Right after I moved, all of my time was spent learning the language. I started reading easy children's books and watching a lot of TV. I would repeat the words I heard, striving to learn and improve. I had always loved studying in general, and I wanted to speak and write the language well. It was not easy for me to learn, but I was determined to do it. Later on, I started to take all the courses possible to improve. In the meantime, the language barrier made life hard. People didn't understand me well because of my heavy accent. I became even more insecure because of my poor pronunciation. I became an introvert because of my inability to hold a decent conversation with others.

Since I had no friends, I felt more alone than ever. Both the fear of being alone and the thought of dying alone consumed me. This was the first time I was truly faced with my loneliness. I felt like I had always been alone, by myself, but now I started feeling loneliness in a deeper way. No matter how many people surrounded me, it didn't matter—my loneliness was deeper than that. You can be in the middle of a huge crowd and still be the loneliest person on this earth. And under certain circumstances, you can experience loneliness on a desert island and yet not feel lonely.

I prayed to my god and received no answer. I had no personal relationship with him. My prayers returned void. I was in a foreign land, alone with my misery and hurt from my past, and I had no one to speak to about anything. There was no one to give me hope. My wounds needed healing, and I had no medicine for them. I was in despair. I started praying to Allah in my own way for him to bring me a husband. (Looking back, I can say that I've learned to be careful what I pray for! If the true God, the Lord Jesus Christ, is not hearing your prayers, then the devil definitely is.)

Shortly after this, I called Maria, my friend from Paris. She couldn't believe that I'd actually done what I had dreamed about doing. It turned out that I was one hour away from where she was now living. We talked on the phone a lot. Then one day, when I told her about my loneliness, she came up with a great idea. She was living with her boyfriend, who had a male friend who was available. I jumped at the idea of meeting someone new. *Oh, I've never had a real boyfriend. Just like in the movies; and he is not from Middle Eastern descent!* I thought. But in my heart I was fearful and saying to myself, *I am ugly, stupid, I cannot even speak the language. He would be very bored with me.*

My friend insisted that I meet him. Afterward, she gave him my phone number. He called me. Oh, it was a mess! My English was terrible, and our conversations on the phone were short. Despite embarrassment and frustration, I tried hard to communicate with my poor English, which I thought was a better option than refusing to practice my English and staying lonely.

One day, he said, "You sound so cute. I would like to meet you."

"Okay," I said, not really understanding. I finally understood what he was saying after he repeated it for the third time. He came to my town and met me at a bar as a blind date. On the phone, we had described to each other how we would look and dress in order to recognize each other. When he finally met me, he said, "Now I can believe how beautiful you are."

"Beautiful? Me?" I must have misunderstood him. But he kept repeating how beautiful, how special I was, many times. I finally got it. He really thought I was beautiful. He was in love with me, and I was in love with him. I was in love with the first person on earth who had found me beautiful, and I didn't have to care for any boundaries anymore. I didn't have my parents, and I had no traditional restrictions. *Hey, we are in America, and everything is permissible,* I thought. I didn't even want to be hard to get. I gave myself to him when we were both drunk. He adored me. I didn't understand his English very well, but I liked him for loving me so much. This was all I needed. Someone who cared for me, who loved me unconditionally and thought that I was beautiful and precious. All I wanted was to be loved.

Deep down, I didn't know if any man could ever give me the kind of love I was longing for. But I was desperate, and I was willing to try just about anything to erase my loneliness.

Chapter 20:

Never Learned

After dating for three months, my new boyfriend and I got married. His family was in shock. I was in shock too. His mother and sister resented me for a long time, but I didn't care about their feelings at the beginning. Then I became offended easily by them. I believed they hated me. And I hated them back. Because of my hatred for them, I had a lot of problems to resolve with my in-laws.

At home, I was happy to be loved for the first time. I was happy that he was working. I felt secure. I was pregnant and was so excited to be having a baby. I partied with my husband even though I was pregnant. I didn't drink alcohol, but I joined him wherever he went. He was a party animal, as he called himself.

There were many misunderstandings in our marriage. One week we were getting along very well together. Then another week, we were having fights all the time. Even so, he never was physically violent toward me, and I was happier than I had ever been. At least, that was what I thought.

Sometimes my emotions of pain and hurt from the past would come to the surface. I would feel down and despairing, believing, *No one will ever truly love me, no one cares, no one understands.* I had deep scars in my heart that were still bleeding. Yet, I was trying to start a new life with someone I barely knew. Now, I look back and see how lost I was in those days. I was wearing many masks to cover up my hurts, anger, sadness, and many more emotions that were hard to face. There were days when all my painful childhood played out before me. There were days when all I could think of was the torture of my previous marriage. I continuously told myself, *I am sick and tired of being a victim. I don't want to be a victim anymore.* Yet I *was* a victim.

Even in the midst of our fights, I wrote many happy letters to my mother in Turkey. My in-laws were starting to accept me a little more, and I felt they had a lot of goodness in them. However, I was not good at relationships. I would become offended easily and would fight back, verbally, with anything I could make up. My immaturity and insecurities, developed over time in my upbringing, destroyed my relationship with my husband's family. We came to a point of complete hatred toward each other.

I looked at a photograph of myself, not smiling, and said to myself, "I am all alone in a foreign country. Instead of them being a family for me, look what they do to me!" I was angry and bitter towards my in-laws because of how I felt they treated me.

After I gave birth to my daughter, Melis, our marriage started to fail little by little. Since I'd become a mother, I was not able to party with my husband or go fishing with him. I was growing more miserable each day, until I became suicidal. I believed I was not good enough for anybody. My husband continued his life of pleasures while I was at home with the baby. Then his addictions started to come to the surface. As I found out more about his habits, I was shocked at my blindness. Deception was his middle name. I started to confront him when he came home in the middle of the night, drunk and under the influence of pot. We fought, screaming and yelling until the sound echoed through the community where we lived. We received warnings many times from different sources.

My husband started to disappear for entire weekends, and sometimes even longer. He was nice when he was sober. When he was drunk, he was verbally abusive and threw things around. Moreover, his addiction to pornography increased more and more. His pornography addiction was the most hurtful of all. Today, many men are slaves to this dark and demonic addiction. It is destroying many lives and many marriages. I know a lot of women are living in complete misery because of their husbands' bondage. The home where there is a pornography is not a home, but a gloomy dungeon. I know the pain and the darkness of it.

Then an idea came to my mind. If my husband converted to Islam, everything would be better. I was still praying to my god in a Muslim way. A Muslim woman I knew gave me an English Koran, and I started to read to him when he was at home. Even when he was sleeping, I whispered suras to him in Arabic. It was no use. He found my religion too depressing for him. Actually, I felt the same way when I read the Koran. But I always found a way to explain things and justify most of the scary scriptures. I just wanted Allah to intervene and take care of everything. I was tired. I was tired of trying to fix everything. I was tired of life. I was tired of trying to reach Allah. I was tired of myself.

I was exhausted, and I just wanted to find a solution.

Chapter 21:

Escaped Again

Miserable and trapped in another bad marriage, I found a way to escape again by studying. I went back to college to advance my command of the English language. Meanwhile, I was evangelizing Islam on the campus. The irony of it hit me even then: I was sharing my faith with others, yet I felt my faith had no power in my life. I completed all the English courses that I could possibly finish. Then I started studying to be a computer specialist.

Meanwhile, I made some friends. One of them, Kara, was very significant in my life. She was a lot older than me, and I became dependent on her for knowledge of many things in regards to the country, community, and people. Kara was skin and bones, so thin it was hard to look at her. She was also a well-known feminist in our community, with a bad reputation of having no values or boundaries with men, and she had lots of confidence—she didn't seem to care how people felt about her. She was a strong defender of women's rights, and she felt that women should live their lives sexually just like men. She found me very naive and uneducated in regards to men, and she designated me as her student to train me to be a tough, feminist woman.

I accepted her training with open arms. *I have done everything right up to now,* I thought, *I've been a good girl and failed; now, I am going to be tough, strong, like a man.*

Kara trained many other women like me, and she destroyed many of marriages with her wicked counsels. Studying and reading horoscopes was her biggest interest. She lived her life based on New Age books and Eastern practices. I was looking for answers. I was wide open to her teaching.

Together, we studied Karma, Zen, and occult religions. I started meditating with her. All of these movements and their doctrines seemed comforting somehow. Later on, I understood that all of the religions, whether Islam or Buddhism or New Age philosophy, offer some kind of temporary relief, peace, and comfort. Otherwise no one would ever follow their practices. However, at the end they leave you empty because they are only substitutes for the real thing.

Kara and I were into reincarnation, Buddhism, and more. In real life, none of these things could heal my wounds or save me from my miseries. But at least I had found something I could hold on to, I thought. I kept doing everything she did and obeyed her as if she was my mother.

Kara was married when I met her. Then she and her husband separated. She found a boyfriend while her husband was traveling overseas and started living with him. I came to visit her and her boyfriend from time to time with my daughter. Her boyfriend, Ari, was an Armenian, from Turkey, with what I thought were mental problems. He was a very nice person, very genuine, but lacking a little in his appearance. He was short and chubby. My friend was skinny as a skeleton. They made a weird couple. But I loved them, and I had compassion for her boyfriend's problem.

One day, Ari described his mental illness to me. He said, "There is something in me, like a burning ball of fire. It is like burning wax inside me. It's completely oppressing me." Then he asked me, "Do you believe in demons?"

"Demons? Yes, I do," I replied. Demons were an accepted reality in Islam. Just talking with him about them was a scary thing for me. I didn't know much about demons; I'd heard about them and the bad spirits, but I always tried to stay away from those subjects. I had enough fears in my life.

He continued, "I feel like I have many of them inside me."

Once, Ari was arrested for driving on the wrong side of the highway. "Demons controlled me," he said. While one of the cops was about to put handcuffs on him, he suddenly pulled out the cop's gun and tried to commit suicide. When he put the gun to his head, the cop punched him in the head and knocked him out.

I felt deeply sorry for Ari, and I prayed some prayers from the Koran in Arabic for his sake. I told him to read the Koran, which he did. But nothing seemed to work. I prayed one of the most powerful scriptures over him. Kara took him to sorcerers, all types of doctors, and even had him try elixirs. But after all these treatments, his situation got worse instead of getting better.

Kara really loved and cared for him. She spent a lot of money trying to get him cured. Some said that he was crazy. Others said that he truly was demon-possessed. In the midst of all this, I started wondering about the truth. What truth was the Truth? Which way was the Way? How could I reach God and know about Him? Were we so filthy, weak, and wicked that He couldn't even care for us? My mind was full of questions, condemnations, and doubts. It felt like wherever I turned, I found only a little relief, and then after a short while, all the problems, struggles, and torment would come flooding back again. I was like a drunk person, and when I became sober, nothing would have changed either internally or on the outside. I had to find the truth—the real truth that could really change things.

Chapter 22:

TV Commercial

One day Kara called me and said that she'd seen a church commercial on TV that said they could cast out demons and heal the sick in Jesus's name. To my shock and anger, she told me that they were getting ready to go to this church. I thought my friends were blaspheming Allah by going to Jesus for help. Jesus was a prophet in Islamic teaching, but they were going to this church to get healed by Jesus. I was angry and confused. Ari didn't believe at that point that anyone could help him, even Jesus. But since she insisted, he agreed to try. They had already spent a lot of money trying to find help for him. When they arrived at the church, a few people were waiting for them as if they had an appointment. Some Christians took them into an office.

Ari asked them, "How much money are you going to charge me?" They answered, "We don't want your money. We would like to pray over you in the name of our Lord Jesus." This was quite a shock for him—he was accustomed to people asking for a lot of money to try to help him. He thought, *Hmmm. No money?* Then he said to them, "Well then, start whenever you wish."

They started praying over him. They laid their hands on him. Then they started crying and weeping and asking Jesus to heal him.

Later he said to me, "Something started happening in my heart at that time. That fireball in my heart started moving and shrinking. I started crying with them. I did not know what was happening, but I felt as if my heart was changing. I started to see that there was hope in the name of Jesus. When they finished praying, one young guy highlighted many verses in a Bible. He gave me the Bible and said, 'Please read these verses.' I went home and started reading them, and then I kept on reading the entire Bible."

Within two weeks, Ari gave his heart to Jesus. He got completely healed and became radical for Christ. He broke off his relationship with my friend, saying that he didn't want to sin anymore. And he started preaching Jesus to us. At that point I was happy that he'd gotten healed, but I was sick of his preaching to me—he was constantly telling me that I was going to hell if I didn't accept Jesus as my Lord. He was really getting on my nerves.

After a few months, Ari went back to Turkey to serve Jesus. He stayed there for a few years, experiencing persecution, insults, and all kinds of harassment. But, he witnessed and ministered to many Muslims.

The separation from her boyfriend was hard on Kara, yet she put her tough female mask on once again. Her divorce finally came through, and she was free again.

Meanwhile, Kara met some Christians. She was miserable and bitter, but looking for answers. She would go back and forth talking about Jesus.

I remember one day she told me on the phone, "I think Jesus is higher than Mohammed." I got angry at her and rebuked her for saying such a thing. And yet, I knew that I was not receiving any help or healing from the religion I had been born into. I felt as if I was in complete darkness. I was hitting myself against the wall like a helpless prisoner. There was no way out. My life meant nothing to me.

My one bright spot, my only source of laughter, was my daughter. Melis was not aware of any of my feelings. She was a happy baby, funny and charming. I was trying to be happy very hard. Yet I was bleeding inside.

Chapter 23:

Dumped on the Highway

Over the next several months, many missionaries knocked on my door to talk about Jesus. I slammed my door in their faces, outraged, believing they were from the devil and not from Allah. I remember yelling at them, "Leave me alone! I do not want your Jesus. If you read the Koran, I will read your Bible." They always infuriated me. They were worshiping three gods—Father, Son, and Holy Spirit—and it was a blasphemy to Allah. Interestingly, I never got angry at the Buddhists or Hindus. But whenever Christians tried to talk to me about their Jesus, I would get extremely angry.

On New Year's Eve, 2000, my husband and I were planning to go to a friend's house for a holiday dinner. I tried my best to look pretty for the occasion. I got Melis ready. I had put on my "happy face" mask like I was so good at doing, but my heart was heavy and emotionally aching. My husband had not come home yet—late as usual when there was any event we had planned for together. He acted like I was not important to him. I was trying to control my tears so I would not ruin my makeup. When I couldn't hold my anger in any longer, I went to the restroom and knelt on the floor. I prayed out loud, screaming "Hear me, my Creator! Hear me, please! Do something about my life, my Maker. Do something. Just do something! I cannot take this anymore. Change my life. Change me!" I yelled this prayer over and over again.

After a long while, my husband finally arrived. He appeared to be intoxicated. I didn't want to go anywhere with him anymore, but he insisted. Instead of going to our friend's house for a New Year's Eve dinner as planned, my husband drove us to another party. He drank more liquor there. Every time I pleaded for him to stop drinking and take us home, I received curses for his answers.

Then he put us back into the car and started to drive toward the place of our original invitation. We were on a four-lane highway, and he started to make zigzags by crossing several lanes back and forth. He was so drunk that sometimes he had to close his eyes and breathe with difficulty. I was crying out loud, telling him that I wanted to drive, but he ignored me.

When we saw a police car approaching us, my husband's driving improved temporarily. I opened my door while the car was moving to try to get the policeman's attention. My husband screamed at me to shut the door. I wanted the cops to notice our strange behavior and stop us. The policeman disappeared without helping us. My husband started punching me. I was screaming. Suddenly he stopped the car, and with my door still opened, he kicked me out. I hit the pavement with a thud. Then he sped away from me, leaving me on the side of the road.

I was in the middle of nowhere. I didn't know what to do or where to go. I wept loudly, trying to pull down my miniskirt and clean up my makeup and take off my earrings. I started to walk toward a highway exit, but I was walking very slowly because of my high heels. Cars were stopping, probably because they thought I was a prostitute on the side of the highway. It was New Year's Eve, and everybody was going to a party. I was subject to their humiliations because I'd been discarded by my husband on the side of the highway.

I looked up to the dark sky and screamed, "Where are you, God? Where are you? What have I done that was so bad I deserve this? Help me! Please help me!"

Right after that, a car stopped a little distance ahead of me. I was praying that there would be a woman in the car. I said, "Please, please it is a woman. If it is a man, he is going to rape me, rob me, or kill me. Please God, let it be a woman."

As I got closer to the car, I could make out a person—a woman in the driver's seat. I blurted out, "It is a woman! It is a woman!" There was a woman in the car as I had prayed!

She opened her car window and asked me what had happened. I told her all the details, sniffing tearfully between my words. She smiled and said, "Listen, I am going to a friend's house for a party. Get in, and I will take you with me." She seemed to be telling the truth—I could see party food and soda in the backseat. But I just looked at her in shock. I didn't know what to do. I felt like a beaten-up dog, ready to receive one more kick. Now someone was offering me help and kindness. It was hard to believe.

I questioned her, "Why? Why would you help me?"

She smiled kindly and said, "What would Jesus do? God sent me to pick you up. Come on and get in, okay?"

Timidly, I got inside her car. She gave me a can of soda to drink and some tissues to clean my face, and she kept telling me, over and over again, that the Lord had incredible, wonderful plans for my life. I hardly knew what to think!

When we arrived at her friend's house, wonderful people started to surround me and express their love and care toward me. They treated me like royalty. I was weeping—for once, with happy tears. I was crying with joy for the overwhelming love I was receiving from these wonderful people. And they didn't even know me!

After dinner, the lady who had picked me up on the deserted highway asked me if I knew anyone I could stay with. I got on the phone and called some of my so-called best friends including Kara, but not one wanted to lend me a helping hand.

Then I remembered a Spanish lady who had taken care of my daughter several times. I knew that she had been through a similar situation to mine. I called her. She didn't speak much English. But she understood me well enough to say, "You are welcome to my house."

So after dinner, the lady who had befriended me took me to my Spanish friend's house. Her name was Norma, and it turned out that she was a strong Christian. She said, *"Mi casa es su casa*—my home is your home." Then she took me to a nice bedroom where I prepared to spend a peaceful night.

The next day, Norma took me to a police station and dropped me off. I told the police what had occurred with my husband. They agreed to protect and escort me home so I could pick up my daughter without harm. When we got to my house, there were already a few police cars in our driveway. My escort and I went inside to find my husband crying, remorseful for what he had done to me last night on the highway.

But I had already made up my mind. I was there to pick up Melis and a few of my belongings. Our home was no longer a safe place for my daughter and me. Without looking back, I was walking away from my second marriage and my second failure.

Chapter 24:

Daughter Near Death

The police were kind enough to take my daughter and me to Norma's house. The first week there, I didn't even take a shower, I was in such darkness and depression. Norma and her daughter, Maria, helped Melis and me as much as they could, even though I wasn't a very good recipient. Under Kara's supervision, I started a new life of partying. She was still my teacher, training me to become like her. When I came back late at night, I would find Norma on her knees praying for me. She was very kind and loving—not condemning, but praying for me. The love and kindness that came from Norma and her daughter made our life change easier on my daughter. They had a swimming pool and a cute dog that Melis played with. She was two-and-a-half years old at that time.

One night, I was blow-drying my hair after taking a shower. My daughter and the dog were playing in the hallway. When I turned off the drier, I noticed that Melis was not around. I was terrified and ran outside to the pool. I saw her, motionless, in the middle of the pool. I froze. I couldn't even move. I was sure that she had drowned. Her body was lying there helpless, and I couldn't face it.

Norma had followed me out, and she jumped into the pool with no hesitation. She pulled my daughter out and laid her body on the ground. I felt like I was dying. My daughter's face was purple. Her little body was just laying there.

Norma had started praying out loud. She was weeping and begging

Jesus to give my daughter's life back to me. She was praying in a different language. It was not Spanish, nor English. It sounded like a language from heaven—a language that I had never heard before.

A moment later, Melis started to come back to life, coughing up water from her lungs. I ran to her and took her in my arms. Then I started to cry hysterically. I turned to Norma, saying, "Thank you! You saved my daughter's life."

She replied in her broken English, "Don't thank me. Thank the One who raised your daughter from death. His name is Jesus."

Because of my doubt and unbelief, I could not rationalize why my daughter was not dead. To my thinking, there was no miracle performed by Jesus. I tried to explain what had happened in my way. But I couldn't even convince myself. Even the Koran accepted that Jesus healed the sick and raised the dead. I remembered the scriptures that I had read about Him. He was a miracle worker. This was all I knew about Him. At that moment, I remembered the childhood dream that He was going to give me eternal life. Had He truly resurrected my daughter?

I thought about Jesus a lot that night.

Chapter 25:

Cramming Session

After few weeks of staying at Norma's house, I knew that I had to find a job. Norma was also going through a divorce. Her husband was a drug dealer and a violent man. She needed help. Even though she never mentioned money, I knew that couldn't live at her home for free.

With only a dollar in my purse and less than a half-tank of gas in my car, I was soon driving to a job interview, trying to locate the actual physical address of the business. Besides my desire to pay Norma, my daughter was in a day care center, and I owed them quite a bit of money. I had put on my best outfit for the interview: a tight, yellow-and-black checkered pants outfit, with a nice long black blazer which made a good contrast with my bleached blonde hair. My high heels were the wrong size, but I tried to make the best of it.

When I look at my old pictures, I know that I didn't look decent in those days. I couldn't see it at the time. I thought my only problem was wearing high-heeled shoes that were not my size!

As I drove, many thoughts were flooding through my mind. After realizing that my college diplomas from my own country were not good enough, I had decided to study to become a computer specialist. That plan had been going well, but then the highway incident happened, and one month before my graduation, I found myself on my own again, looking for a job so that I could survive with a two-year-old girl. I begged a lady with the placement center at my school to get me a job interview so I could work. After all, I was one of the hardest working students in my class.

Taking pity on me, she gave me an address for a job interview, but not the name of the company. "I am not sure if you will get this job, since you haven't completed your classes yet. But you are the best student so far. I am sure you will be able to manage this new job if you are chosen for the position." This unnamed company she was sending me to was looking for someone who was proficient in the Access program for computers.

I shook my head a little, trying to clear it as I thought back on the last few days. Eager to get the job, I had gone to my school's bookstore to see what they had available about this program. I asked the cashier, "What do you have for Access?" He pointed out the shelves that displayed many help books and videotapes on the subject. I wanted to get all of them, and I planned to study them all that weekend. But I had no money to pay for them. I kept staring at these resources.

The cashier was watching me. He said, "This is a difficult program to learn. Access is more complicated than the others."

"I know," I said. "I do not have too much time to learn this program. I have a job interview this Monday. They need someone who is qualified with this program."

"That's not possible," he said. "It will take you months to master the program."

"I must try. I really need the job. I have a two-year-old daughter, and I just became a single mother." In desperation, I tried to gain his sympathy. All I wanted from this guy was his pity.

It worked. "Well, then," he said, "get whichever you want."

"I want all of these videotapes and these books."

He blurted out, "You are crazy! Do you think you will be able to learn all these in two days?"

"And two nights," I added. "If I sleep only for two hours a day, I can make it. I have done it before."

"That is insane," he said.

"I have a little problem, though," I said.

"What is your problem other than that you're mental?"

I tried to sound confident, even though I was embarrassed. "I don't have money to pay for them."

"Then there is nothing I can do for you," he said seriously.

I said, "But I am desperate to find a job. Can I just borrow them?"

"Listen, this is a bookstore not a library!"

"I know," I said, "but I must study them. Come on. You probably never needed help. I need help. I will return them on Monday. I will give you a copy of my driver's license, and I will sign an agreement that I owe you a certain amount of money if I do not return them."

He paused for a moment.

"Please! I am begging you."

"Well," he said, "only if you promise to go out with me."

I thought, *He is so disgusting.* But I didn't say that. I said, "Yes, I promise I will go out with you."

Then he gave me all the books and videotapes I desired. I hated him at that moment so much that I could hardly say, "Thank you." Just the thought of going out with him was repulsive to me.

"Remember," he said, "you promised." He smiled at me lustfully. I just wanted to vomit.

"Yes, of course," I replied, knowing that I would prefer to die than keep my promise to him.

I picked up every resource on the Access program, including all the help books and videos on the shelving unit that I had pointed out to him. Then I rushed over to a friend's house to use her computer to study all weekend. I didn't even have a computer of my own.

Now it was Monday, and my furious weekend of study was about to pay off—or not. Finally, I came across a gas station and the building mentioned on the scribbled scrap of paper. All I needed to find now was parking and the person who was going to interview me. The paper said his name was Rudy.

I parked my car and looked in the mirror one more time to retouch the bright pink color on my lips. I looked like a zombie. I had used a lot of makeup to cover the dark circles around my eyes, but there was no hope for the puffiness. My high heels were hurting me terribly, but I had nothing else to wear. My hands were sweating with nervousness, and my heart was beating rapidly. I told myself, *You must look calm. You must look confident. Don't you ever blow this interview, Isık.*

I walked into the building and took the elevator. When the elevator door opened on the third floor, I saw a huge sign that said "Millennium Church." *This cannot be,* I said to myself. *Church of Millennium? This is a church? I can't believe this!*

Before the elevator door closed again, an old lady with a nice smile asked, "Do you need help, my dear?" She entered the elevator and with one hand pressed the button to keep the door open. I was trapped.

Chapter 26:

New Job at a "Church Company"

How could this happen? I was asking myself. *A church? What am I doing here?* I was a Muslim—actually a backslidden Muslim. But still, once a Muslim, always a Muslim. *There is no hope for me in this place. They will ask me a religious question, and I will fail. If they know I am a Muslim, they will never hire me.*

The nice old lady said, "You are at the right place, dear. Are you looking for Rudy?"

"Yes," I asked, "how did you know?"

"He is interviewing people today. Come in. Have a seat. I will go and tell him you are here."

All I could think was, *I need this job more than anyone else.*

Then Rudy appeared. He was a well-dressed, nice-looking man with a smile on his face, and he walked quickly toward me. "You must be Isık," he said. "Did I say your name correctly?"

"Yes, sir," I said.

"Please, follow me. Did you find the address easily?"

"Yes, sir," I said again.

He smiled. "Come into my office and have a seat."

His office was big and nicely decorated. It had a beautiful bay view, but the scenery did nothing to calm my nerves.

He started the interview me by asking, "So you are from Turkey?"

"Yes, sir," I answered. I knew I sounded repetitive, but I just didn't know what else to say.

"Your resume is very impressive," he continued. "So you worked in Turkey and in several countries of Europe in very high positions? You have a post study in business, am I correct?"

I told him yes.

"Very well; very well. So you have a family here with you?" Rudy asked.

I responded, "No, all I have is my two-year-old daughter."

He paused. "Are you divorced?"

"Yes, sir," I said.

"Is he paying your child support? Is he a good father to your daughter?"

Why does he care? I thought. This interview was not going at all as I had expected.

"He pays child support time to time. I guess he is learning to be a good dad."

"Good," Rudy said, and he smiled kindly. This job interview got stranger by the minute!

"I see that you are also a computer specialist. Is that correct?"

"Yes, sir," I replied, glad that I finally had something else to say. "I am efficient in Microsoft applications, networking, and also Photoshop."

"That is excellent," he said with a smile. "Do you live close by?"

"Not now," I said, "but if I am hired, I will be moving closer."

"That's good. That's good," he affirmed.

I have never met anyone so positive, I thought.

Rudy sat back and folded his hands. "My only concern is that you are overqualified for this position!" he said.

My heart jumped. "That is all I have been hearing, sir, in my job interviews. I do not mind being overqualified. I need to pay my bills, sir. I need this job!"

Rudy nodded. "Let me contact our vice president. He will ask you a few more questions."

After he left, a few minutes passed which felt like eternity to me. Then he came back with another nice gentleman who was also smiling at me. Rudy stayed for this next interview, settling into another chair beside the desk.

"Hi, my name is Paul," the newcomer said. "I'm joint vice president here, along with Rudy and one other gentleman. You are Isık—did I say your name right?"

"Yes, sir," I replied.

"So Rudy told me you are very good with computers, is that correct? Do you know Access?" "Yes, sir," I replied, deciding not to say anything about the exhausting weekend I had just endured. After all, they didn't need to know how I had learned it!

"How well do you know this program?" Paul asked.

"Very well, sir," I replied confidently. It was true.

Then he started asking me a lot of questions about the program. I answered them one by one, and I could see more and more satisfaction on his face.

At last he sat back, smiling. "Well, we have been interviewing many individuals for the last couple of weeks. You have been the most knowledgeable person we have interviewed for this position so far."

"Thank you sir," I replied. Then I relaxed a little and smiled. "I learned the program last weekend."

"Yeah, right! You are also very funny!" Paul laughed. "When can you start?"

"Tomorrow," I said, trying not to show the tremendous relief that was flooding my veins.

"Tomorrow it is, then. Congratulations!"

"Thank you, sir. Thank you, thank you! I will not disappoint you."

My legs didn't feel quite steady beneath me as I stood up. At the same time as I was seeing a glimpse of hope, I was nervous and fearful. What would happen if I messed this up? I was also excited that I had been given an opportunity. I didn't know at moment that the opportunity given to me was going to change my life completely.

Rudy and Paul both shook my hand, and then Rudy walked with me outside the office. I was about to get on the elevator again when he said, "Isık, every morning we have a Bible study for the staff. It is optional. I wish you would join us."

I stiffened and thought, *Oh no!* But I said to Rudy, "I will try to make it."

"Good, I will see you tomorrow then. But you must come a half an hour earlier before work. You will like it, I promise."

As I left, I couldn't believe that I had just agreed to attend a Bible study. I couldn't even believe I'd been hired by a company that had the word "church" in its name. *Now I will be working in a Christian company. These Christians are everywhere!*

Chapter 27:

Bible Study on the Job

If any one of you is without sin, let him be the first to throw a stone at her (John 8:7).

For hours I struggled with myself about going to the Bible study at work. I was overcome with guilt. Before I left for my first day, I prayed in my Muslim way, "Allah God, I am a Muslim, and I will always be. Going into that Bible study will not make me a Christian. I will just go inside that room and receive the good things. I will not listen to anything about Jesus that they are saying. They are worshiping Him as if He is God, and it is a big sin. I know this. Please forgive me and do not count this as a sin. I am just going to be there to please my boss."

This would be the first Bible study I had attended, and I was struggling inside myself. At one time, when I was younger, I'd thought I had all the answers and that I had figured out how everything worked. But now I had failed in every area of my life. I was twenty-eight years old and going through a second divorce. My daughter was two years old, and I was in depression and facing the darkest days of my life. I needed some kind of answers, some kind of hope. But I didn't want to go to the study. I told myself that I hated Christians. They worshiped a man. They blasphemed my god and His oneness. I would never tell my parents that I was going to such a thing—they'd think I was a loser for sure. I even thought, *They are going to try to brainwash me.*

To make matters worse, I hadn't told my new bosses that I was a Muslim. I had just needed the job so desperately.

But as I entered the room designated for Bible study, I felt such a peace. It was totally unexpected. I couldn't understand the calmness and peace that were in that room. Nobody was talking. Everybody was quiet, like they were all feeling it—and I could feel it too. I thought before I came to work that I would be expecting all negative feelings: guilt, condemnation, unforgiveness, bitterness, anger. But there was such an overwhelming peace filling that room.

Allen, the president of the company, was also a preacher and a pastor. His wife, Alice, was there too. Both he and his wife had a glow on their faces. He opened up the study with a prayer. I couldn't help saying to myself that it was a beautiful and a humble prayer. But I was supposed to hate it. I was supposed to say, *These are evildoers, man worshipers. They are idolaters.* Oh, I was destined for hell now!

Pastor Allen said, "Let's turn in our Bibles to John, chapter 8, starting with verse 1."

Let's turn in our Bibles? I thought. *I do not have a Bible.* I had been told that the Bible was evil. It was all a big lie. It was changed. The Koran was the perfect book that everybody had to study in my country of Turkey.

Everybody in that room had a Bible except me. Alice was sitting next to me with her Bible open. She looked at me kindly and smiled, whispering, "We'll share." I thought that I had never seen such a beautiful face before. But this was a different kind of beauty. I couldn't understand why she looked at me with eyes that seemed to say, "I love you." At that very moment, I just wanted to cry. I said to myself thoughtfully, *This cannot be. She doesn't know me. How can she love me? Nobody loves me. Nobody! Even Allah; even my own family; how can this stranger love me? She doesn't know that I am a wretch. I am no good for anybody. I am cursed.* I just wanted to cry. I wanted to weep so desperately. I had never used so much effort in my life to keep back my tears.

While I was in the midst of this storm of feelings, Pastor Allen started reading the passage from the Bible with a gentle voice. As he began, I steeled my heart to reject the message. I told myself, *He doesn't know the truth. He is reading a lie.*

Yet, the passage of Scripture captured my attention:

> *But Jesus went to the Mount of Olives. At dawn he appeared again in the temple courts, where all the people gathered around him, and he sat down to teach them. The teachers of the law and the Pharisees brought in a woman caught in adultery. They made her stand before the group and said to Jesus, "Teacher, this woman was caught in the act of adultery. In the Law Moses commanded us to stone such women. Now what do you say?"*
>
> *They were using this question as a trap, in order to have a basis for accusing him.*
>
> *But Jesus bent down and started to write on the ground with his finger.*
>
> *When they kept on questioning him, he straightened up and said to them, "If any one of you is without sin, let him be the first to throw a stone at her."*
>
> *Again he stooped down and wrote on the ground.*
>
> *At this, those who heard began to go away one at a time, the older ones first, until only Jesus was left, with the woman still*

standing there. Jesus straightened up and asked her, "Woman, where are they? Has no one condemned you?"

"No one, sir," she said.

"Then neither do I condemn you," Jesus declared. "Go now and leave your life of sin," (John 8:1–11).

I couldn't believe what I was hearing. *This is ridiculous,* I thought. *This woman was caught in the act of adultery. Can you believe how shameful it was then, and how it is now! Yet Jesus didn't condemn her. He forgave her. This is a bunch of baloney. She had to be stoned. She was a worthless, adulterous woman.*

Allen started explaining this passage while I went back in my mind as far as ten years ago, to the day I went to an orphanage as a volunteer in Istanbul. I was going there to teach them Islam and reading them stories from literature. I was eighteen years old at that time, and I had so much compassion for those orphans. Even though I was very young, they all called me "Mother." This had broken my heart. I wanted to adopt all of them.

I remembered one particular visit especially: on this day, there was a Muslim minister in charge of children's religious education with me in the class. He was teaching the fundamentals of Islam on the subject of adultery and forgiveness. Then he gave time for the children to ask questions and discuss these topics.

One of the boys raised his hand. He was about eleven years old. The boy shouted with uncontrollable anger, "My mother was an adulterous. After she gave birth to me, she left me here. If I ever find her, I will kill her for that. I will never forgive her; therefore, Allah will never forgive her either. Oh, how much I want to kill her!"

I was in shock at this little boy's angry comments. Meanwhile, the Muslim minister quickly picked up the topic from where the little boy had left off. I was hoping that he was going to correct the boy for this outburst. Yet, the minister joined the boy in his anger. He said, "Your mother should be stoned to death. You have every right to kill her, I believe. She doesn't deserve any forgiveness from you, from us, or from Allah. She is destined for hell."

The orphans shouted in agreement with this minister. I was struck by his statements, representing hatred and unforgiveness. The minister repeated, "The woman who commits adultery must be stoned to death."

". . . Isık. Your name *is* Isık . . . am I saying your name correctly?"

Pastor Allen was repeating my name. *Oh my goodness,* I thought, jarring back to the Bible study. I didn't realize that I had been daydreaming . . . and I had raised my hand to ask a question without realizing it! *Oh, I am so stupid.* But it was too late. I said out loud, "How could this be? How can Jesus forgive that adulterous woman? She was caught in the very act of adultery. She was worthless. She had to be stoned to death."

I couldn't believe I had objected to a Bible teaching on my first day of work. *They are going to fire me,* I thought. But Pastor Allen smiled kindly and said, "Isık, that woman, that adulterous woman whom you just called worthless, was worthy in the eyes of our Lord Jesus. Jesus loved her unconditionally, so much that if she was the only person on this earth, Jesus would have come and died on the cross for her."

His gentle answer pierced my heart. Now I was not able to control my tears. I thought to myself, *I am that sinful woman. I am worthless, but how can Jesus sees me worthy? How can he love me?*

Chapter 28:

Absolute God

That first study, with its strange and beautiful story of forgiveness, changed something in me. I couldn't wait for the next morning when we would study the Bible again. I started falling in love with the Jesus I had hated so much before. Still, I didn't understand the concept of Jesus being the Son of God. I trembled at the idea of this blasphemy, directed at my god, Allah, who was called the "Absolute One God." *How could it be that God could have a son? This is a terrible mistake,* I said to myself many times.

Yet, I was very attracted to this teaching of Jesus. I wanted to comprehend it. I wanted to understand His unconditional love. I had searched for this type of love while I lived as a young adult in Turkey. I had written essays about it and spent hours thinking about it. Unfortunately, the Muslims did not comprehend unconditional love. The Turkish men I dated left me feeling unworthy of myself. I thought I had done everything right in my life, and as a result I was victimized by men. Because I was treated disrespectfully, I decided to be morally bad myself. Kara, my best friend at the time, became my worst enemy later—and perhaps she was even then. She said, "I will teach you how to be bad and how to deal with men. You will live your life like a man." She set me up with guys. She was very proud of that she slept with more than a hundred men. I partied with her and them and lived the lowest life possible. I was so thirsty for love, but no relationship was able to satisfy that thirst.

Jesus answered the Samaritan woman, "If you knew the gift of God and who it is that asks you for a drink, you would have asked him and he would have given you living water."

"Sir," the woman replied, "you have nothing to draw with and the well is deep. Where can you get this living water? Are you greater than our father Jacob, who gave us the well and drank from it himself, as did also his sons, and his flocks and herds?"

Jesus answered, "Everyone who drinks this water will be thirsty again, but whoever drinks the water I give him will never thirst. Indeed, the water I give him will become in him a spring of water welling up to eternal life," (John 4:10–14).

After my second marriage, with Kara's help I let several men use and abuse me while deceiving myself that I was using them to change myself into a tough girl. For a short while, I went from one bar to another. I became bitter, I felt like a failure, and I was lost. Shortly after that, my best buddy became my worst enemy. Kara came into my life as the deceiver, and then she became the accuser. She accused me of things I hadn't done along with things that I had, and her jealousy led us to separate. This separation helped me more than it hurt me, though it did hurt badly at the time.

She slandered me and left me as an outcast in the community. I learned to remain silent about the accusations. Crying silently, I was left with no one, no friend, and it felt like I had lost everything. All of this had happened shortly before I was given this job.

Now I was going into this Bible study with my broken pieces, hurt, shame, guilt, misery, depression, and many other dark feelings. I felt that I was not a good Muslim anymore. How could I be, even if I hadn't done so much wrong? The Koran's list of dos and don'ts was too long. I never could be sure of being accepted by Allah. I felt that I was not good enough for anyone or anything. I felt dirty, a failure, abandoned. I cried myself to sleep many nights.

I was lost as a mother as well. I blamed others, I blamed myself, I blamed the world and Allah for my cursed destiny. Wherever I turned, I was betrayed, despised, and forgotten. *Yes, there are winners and losers in this life,* I thought. But I was on the losers' side.

With all of that going on in my life and heart, I suddenly felt that this morning Bible study was my only hope. I could barely see a light there. I believed I was not good enough to be there, yet I was receiving unconditional love from both the pastor and his wife. Every word they spoke and read from the Bible touched and started to heal my severely bleeding wounds. My wounds were deep. Every word that was spoken in this Bible study was healing balm to my wounds and scars. I tried to hide my tears from the rest of the members of the group. But I could not hide them from myself. I had found hope, and slowly, it was beginning to change me.

Chapter 29:

Confusion about the Trinity

For the message of the cross is foolishness to those who are perishing, but to us who are being saved it is the power of God (1 Corinthians 1:18).

Though I was learning more and more at the Bible study, I didn't understand the meaning of the cross. "What is so significant about the cross?" I asked myself many times. I thought, *These Christians are trying to make too much out of this cross.*

When I finally became a Christian, I understood that the cross was God's love message to all mankind. I learned that Jesus loved me unconditionally. No matter how bad and terrible I was, He loved me with an everlasting love. God also said to me, "I talked to my creation through prophets; I went to earth in human flesh and delivered my love message to people myself. I wanted them to know they have a Creator who loves them. I went to earth and became just like one of them, and I delivered my love message to them by dying on the cross for them."

But it took me some time to come to that understanding. At first, it was too good to be true—this "Jesus loves" message. If I could ever have imagined a loving God, a caring God and Creator, it would be Jesus. Yet, I was not ready to surrender my life to Him. I was tormented between my will and His. My will was comprised of my family, my country, and my culture. Islam had been my religion from birth. In order to convert and become a Christian, I would first have to deny myself, my past, and everything that was connected to me. What it all boiled down to was that I would have to turn my back on everything I had known and follow Jesus Christ. This was too much for me to handle.

The other aspect of the Christian message that I did not understand was the concept of God the Father, Son, and Holy Spirit being united as one in the Trinity. I'd thought that Christians worshiped three gods. I was told by Rudy in a private conversation after one of our Bible studies that the Trinity was all one God.

He said, "Isık, the Bible says God created man in His own image. So isn't man made up of body, soul, and spirit? The body, soul, and spirit are all one unit that is man. It is the same way with God. The Trinity is all one God. God's existence is in the form of three persons, but He is one God."

Although this approach was foreign, still, it started to make sense to me. But the change was taking place in my heart more than in my head. This love of Jesus was piercing through my heart, through my very being, and touching the secret parts of my soul. I became conscious of the difference between darkness and light and how my eternal destiny was being formed inside me. I started to worry about my soul's eternal salvation.

Yet, even though I was being bombarded by all these concepts, I was not ready to surrender to the Lord God. I was not ready to lose control of myself, scared to lose control and fall into the arms of a Christian God. My uneasiness became a daily struggle as I grew ever more aware of this tug-of-war. I had no peace. I was so used to living with my problems, from one mess to the next, but now, I was aware of being restless. My true purpose on earth and my eternal destiny were facing me every moment.

I knew that I had to lose control of myself and divorce myself from the Islamic religion. I felt that I had been wise in my own ways up till now as a Muslim. I'd had answers for everything, for everybody, and for every situation. But my way of thinking was not saving me from the deep, dark pit of hell. It wasn't even saving me from my own failures.

My own wisdom couldn't provide the saving power for cleansing my dirty soul. My own wisdom was not good enough to change me or give me a new life with a new heart.

> *For the wisdom of this world is foolishness in God's sight. As it is written: "He catches the wise in their craftiness,"*
> (1 Corinthians 3:19).

I knew now that I had to surrender all my knowledge. I had to forget about my college degrees, my studies, and the thousands of books I had read. Everything had to be discarded. Everything in me had to be disowned in order to gain everything from the Lord. I had to lose it completely to win it all.

> *Then Jesus said to His disciples: "If anyone would come after me, he must deny himself and take up his cross and follow me,"*
> (Matthew 16:24).

There was this little voice, a gentle voice in me saying, "Surrender . . . surrender . . . surrender."

I fought against this soft voice. I resisted Him, the Lord. I rejected Him. For many nights I would cry myself to sleep.

The same voice may be calling out your name today and saying, "Surrender . . . surrender . . ." If you just surrender, if you just give your heart to Him today, right now, you will never be the same. Can you hear it?

You may have been a believer for a long time. You may even be serving in a church. And deep inside you know there are things in your heart that you have not given up, and a gentle voice is whispering into your soul, "Surrender . . . surrender . . ."

I was on the verge of losing everything. And when I did, I could not even imagine how much I would find to replace it.

Chapter 30:

With Man, Impossible; With God, Possible

Jesus looked at them and said, "With man this is impossible, but not with God; all things are possible with God,"
(Mark 10:27).

The Bible tells a story about a crippled beggar.

One day Peter and John were going up to the temple at the time of prayer.

Now a man crippled from birth was being carried to the temple gate called "Beautiful," where he was situated everyday to beg from those going into the temple courts.

When he saw Peter and John about to enter, he asked them for money. Peter looked straight at him, as did John. Then Peter said "Look at us!" So the man gave them his full attention, expecting to get something from them. Then Peter said: "Silver and gold I do not have, but what I have I give you. In the name of Jesus Christ of Nazareth, walk." Taking him by the right hand, he helped him up and instantly the man's feet and ankles became strong. He jumped to his feet and began to walk. Then he went with them into the temple courts, walking, and jumping and praising God.

When all the people saw him walking and praising God, they recognized him as the same man who used to sit begging at the temple gate called "Beautiful", and they were filled with wonder and amazement at what had happened to him (Acts 3:1–10).

Silver and gold I do not have, but in the name of Jesus
Christ of Nazareth, walk.
Silver and gold I do not have, but in the name of Jesus
Christ of Nazareth, see.
Silver and gold I do not have, but in the name of Jesus
Christ of Nazareth, be delivered.
In the name of Jesus!

The name of Jesus Christ is the name above all names. Why? Because all authority in heaven and earth was given to Him. He is the first, and He is the last. He is the Son of God. Nobody, nobody can go to the Father, God Almighty, without going by way of Jesus Christ, His Son.

I was that crippled beggar. And I rose up and walked.

Nothing is impossible with God. Nothing!

Just believe!

It took the story of another "cripple" to get me to really pay attention. Rudy, my boss and a man of God, would give the Lord the credit all day long at my work. I would look at my boss with criticism and say to myself, *Heck, what does he know? He looks rich and sharp. He has a wonderful family, car, this and that. He has everything. Of course he praises God all the time. He did not go through the things that I have been through. He has no idea what life is really about. He dresses very sharp. He looks successful. Here I am. Look at me, I am a failure.*

Rudy talked to me about God's unconditional love, how Jesus came to earth in human flesh and died on the cross for our sins so we could have eternal life. I stopped him and said, "You do not know me. I am a wicked woman. I am trash. If you really knew me, you wouldn't talk to me or even look me in the eyes—that's how wicked I am."

He smiled at me kindly and said, "Let me tell you who I was."

While I listened in stunned silence, he told me, "Ten years ago, I was a drug addict, homeless, and a bum. I used to sleep on the streets or in junkyards. I ate from garbage cans, stole from people, and was beaten up by others. One day, I saw a man, sharp-looking, wearing an expensive business suit just like I am wearing right now. He was carrying a nice business briefcase. I was just a beggar on the street. He didn't notice me. He was going to his car by crossing the street. I looked at him for one second and dreamed that I was in his place, cleaned up in a nice suit with a briefcase. Then I said to myself, 'Yeah, right.' I laughed at my stupidity. Still, I could not help looking at him in admiration. He looked important and respected. I again dreamed that I saw myself clean and professionally dressed in a business suit.

"Then I rebuked myself again: 'Yeah, right, that's impossible, you dumb beggar. You are a fool. Impossible! Do you get it? It is impossible.' I removed my eyes from him and looked down at my dirty feet. Then I suddenly noticed a small, dusty Bible between my feet. I picked it up quickly and opened it up carelessly. The first passage that I ever read out of the Bible was the following: 'With man this is impossible, but with God, all things are possible.' I just looked at the words for a few minutes. 'With man this is impossible, but with God, all things are possible'—all things. I read it again and again. I threw away the Bible and started walking down the street with no shoes on and in my filthy outfit. I walked for about a mile. I was still imagining myself as that businessman I saw earlier.

"Suddenly my desperation to find the truth hit me like a lightning bolt. I started running back, screaming, desperate to find the Bible. People were looking at me like I was a crazy beggar.

"I found the Bible. I found my Bible that I had kicked and thrown away. I sat down on the sidewalk and started reading. I read for what seemed hours. I was not a good reader, but God started to give me a new understanding. Tears were rolling down my dirty face. My heart was beating so fast."

He paused for a moment in his story. He was in tears.

"Then what happened?" I asked. "Please, please, you've got to tell me more."

He said, "I bowed down to the ground, weeping. I said, 'Oh God, I do not know how to do this. I have never prayed before, You know. But Lord, now I can see with understanding. I am not stupid anymore. Oh, big God, have mercy on me. Help me, Jesus. I am asking You to be my God. I believe You are the true God. Please accept me. I am begging You.'

"I was on my face on the dirty sidewalk. I asked Jesus to come into my heart. I was weeping bitterly. Then I asked God. 'What do I do now? What do I do?'

"I heard this inner voice come alive in me and say, 'Walk in the direction you are facing now. Go! Knock on the first church door that you come to.' I walked about two miles. I was very hungry and thirsty. But I still looked for that church. Something was happening in my heart. I had so much joy. I had hope. Then, finally, I saw a church and knocked on the door. A man in maintenance clothes opened it. I told him what had happened. He took me in, fed me, gave me a place to sleep and shower. He brought me clean clothes. Moreover, I was mentored by him.

"I started working in the church as a maintenance man. Then I started working in the church office. Another brother trained me in bookkeeping. Then I went to college for the long haul and graduated with an accounting degree.

"When I started working for my first company, I realized that my work ethic was not up to date. I was fired from about seventy jobs, but I never gave up."

As he finished his story, I had to pick up my drooping jaw. I could hardly believe what I'd just heard. My boss had just proven to me by his story that I was not the only one who'd had a rotten life up till now. This beggar's testimony belonged to my boss!

Just think, I thought reflectively, *he is a vice president of a multimillion dollar company. Man can fail many times, but he is not a failure until he gives up for good. So I will not give up. Things are impossible with man, but with God all things are possible. With God all things are possible!*

Then he told me, "Isık, I know how you feel. I have been there myself. I had no self-worth, and I was wicked. But Jesus changed everything for me. When He touches you, He changes you. You just must surrender your life to Him."

From that time, I began to realize the truth that I am still talking about today: God takes our junk and turns it into a masterpiece.

Chapter 31:

Proper Boss

At that time in my life, no one had a greater impact on me than Rudy. He was a joyful, decent man who loved his wife and children dearly. Even more than that, Rudy had told me he was in love with his God, Jesus, very much. And his whole life proved it to be true.

Even though he was a vice president, he was humble and gentle in the spirit. And as a pleasant surprise, he was very proper with women, including me. In the past I was used and abused by men. Rudy's only interest in me was to introduce me to his Savior, who could rescue my dying soul. In all of my encounters with him at work, we were in his office alone only one time. There was a young man at work, David, who loved Jesus as much as Rudy did. Rudy would call David into his office as a third person whenever I was asked to come in. He was always very careful about proper appearances, leaving no room for any misunderstandings. And he was a very transparent person in regard to his own imperfections.

Every time I made a mistake at work, I thought Rudy would fire me, but instead, he showed me mercy and grace. I had never met anyone so gracious.

One day, I asked Rudy why he was so gracious. He said that he was displaying the mercy that he had received from Jesus. He would praise Jesus all day long, until it got on my nerves! I was jealous of his relationship with his God—after all, my god had never given me reason to praise Him all day. However, I knew that Rudy was not perfect in any way, and he never pretended to be. He was a real person who was honest about himself and his failures. That was one reason why I was interested in listening to him when he talked about Jesus.

One day, a salesman called for him. Usually the operator would screen his calls. But this call got past the front desk. I listened to him diplomatically trying to get rid of the salesman on the phone. Then he got upset and hung up. It didn't strike me as anything. But after a few minutes, he left his office to go to the operator who screened his calls and tried to find out the salesman's phone number. Then Rudy really surprised me. Before I knew it, he had called the salesman back. I could hear him say, "I just called you back to apologize. I was rude. I am sorry." I am sure this salesman was in shock as much as I was—maybe even more.

Then he started to talk to him about Jesus. I could hear him saying, "Thank you. You are very gracious. But you know, because of my faith in Jesus, I had to treat you better. I had to be more loving, because God loves you, my friend. I called you to tell you that."

Between Rudy's example on the outside and voice calling "Surrender" on the inside, I didn't think I could hold out against God much longer. And I was right.

Chapter 32:

My Surrender

After a month or two of working at Millennium Church, I woke up one morning wishing that I was dead. I had many bills to pay and a huge debt from the divorce process. My income was not enough to even put food on the table some days. Many days, my meals were Melis's leftovers. I was struggling financially, emotionally, and spiritually. That morning, so many negative thoughts were going through my mind: I was tired of this life. I was tired of myself. My life looked like a failure. I knew that I would not be able to pay the rent at the end of that week. Everything was falling apart.

My three-year-old daughter was sleeping on a small mattress on a floor. She looked like an angel. Tears rolled down my cheeks as I looked at her. In my thoughts, I said, *Anyone could be a better mother. She deserves someone better than me.* I had failed in every area of my life. I had failed in two marriages. I had failed in motherhood. I had failed in taking care of my finances in a right way, ending up broke and in debt. I had failed as a daughter. My parents were ashamed of my divorces. I had failed Allah. He hated me.

That morning was gray and dark, and the shadows covered me like a thick blanket. I was lonely. I felt like a complete outcast. To myself I said, *Life is not worth living. I want to die. I am not able to live this kind of life. It is not for me.* I started dreaming about dying and planning ways to commit suicide. I hugged my baby daughter with tears rolling down my cheeks. She woke up, smiling at me as if everything was going to be okay. I kissed her and kissed her. Then I dressed her and fed her as if it was the last morning we would be together.

Then I took her to her day care. After that, I went to work and started to enter data on my computer, but I could only work for a short time before I went to the restroom to cry. Restroom breaks were an unofficial part of my daily schedule so that I could cry, pray to my god in my own way, and wipe my tears afterward. Then I cleaned my face and went back to my desk like nothing had ever happened.

A voice from the darkness was whispering in my ears, "You are a loser. Your life will never get better. You will always be in a big mess. Oh, what a failure you are! Nobody will want you. Your daughter will hate you." I walked with my head hung down, like a hunchback. The heaviness that had lingered over me since I woke up that morning was now unbearable. I ran again to the restroom. I looked in the mirror and cried and cried. I pitied myself. I hated myself. Everything was hopeless for me.

Then I started asking God, "Why are You forsaking me? Why are You abandoning me? Have mercy on me! What have I done that was so bad to deserve this kind of a life? How did my life turn into trash like this? Here I am knocking. Are You going to open? Everybody has it all together but me. I want to be like them. But I don't know how!"

Then I cleaned my face and waited a few minutes so that my face would look normal and not look like I had been crying. I returned to my desk as if nothing had happened and concealed the storm raging in my heart.

The next thing I knew, Rudy called me into his office. I thought to myself, *Okay. He knows about my restroom visits, and he is going to fire me. Well, again, I am a loser.* I went into his office trembling. Seriously, he said, "Isık, please close the door and have a seat." My heart sank even lower. He never had his office door shut with a member of the opposite sex. I was so sure that he was going to fire me and he didn't want me to be embarrassed.

He said, "Isık, I know this will sound very weird to you. I have never done this before. But I want you to know, my Lord Jesus just told me that He heard your prayer. He knows about your misery. Not only does He know about it, but He also cares for you. He understands. He wants me to tell you that you are not forsaken or abandoned. He loves you, and He wants to take over your mess. Jesus wants me to ask you, will you surrender your life to Him?"

I didn't have to think for a second. I fell on my face and wept uncontrollably. I choked out "Yes" in the midst of my sobs. Then I said, "Yes, Jesus, come into my life and take over. I am sorry for my mistakes. Please forgive me and be my Lord." Suddenly, something happened. In my spirit, I saw a light. Then the Lord's presence seemed to engulf me. I felt Jesus embracing me and pouring down His love on me.

There was a light at the end of my tunnel at last. I knew that I was not alone anymore. If I fell, I knew He would pick me up. At that moment, I received a new heart and a new life. Such joy entered my heart that I had never known before. I met Jesus on my road to Damascus. I met Jesus at the end of my crossroads. And I knew that I was never going to be the same again.

> *At the cross, at the cross, where I first saw the light,*
> *And the burden of my heart rolled away,*
> *It was there by faith I received my sight,*

And now I am happy all the day!
(from "Alas, and Did My Savior Bleed?"
by Isaac Watts, 1707.)

From that day on, Jesus Christ became my Master.

Jesus touched my eyes and healed my blindness. He healed my wounded soul and broken heart. He turned my mess into a message for Him. He took my trash and turned it into a treasure. He rescued my soul. I am eternally thankful. I found the truth, and the truth set me free. I found the peace and joy I had always longed for. Jesus saved my life.

That day, I went to work as the devil's little toy and left as the King's daughter. There were many times in my past as a Muslim woman when I had been approached by Christian people about accepting Jesus as my Savior. I had rejected them every time. But after I prayed in Rudy's office for the Lord to come into my life—He did!

The grass looked greener and the sky looked more blue than ever. I was filled with such joy that I wanted to run through the streets and hug and kiss everyone on my way. Truly, in that day, God rescued my soul.

Chapter 33:

Another Visitation from Jesus

After I invited Jesus into my heart in Rudy's office, I went to the day care to pick up my daughter. Her teacher looked at me as if I might not be the same person who had dropped her off that morning—and I wasn't! I was laughing for the first time with an overwhelming joy. I kissed Melis perhaps a hundred times. I hugged her. I carried her in my arms. She gave me a big smile.

We went home. I didn't care about the bills or the rent that was due. I was so happy that my heart could not contain it. I slept beautifully, with the assurance that we were in Jesus's care. My daughter and I were God's children, and He was going to take care of us. I slept in tremendous peace with my child in my arms.

The next day, I went to work as a different person. I just wanted to let the world know that I was free. The one whom the Son sets free is free indeed! I went to work early to participate in the employees' Bible study and prayer meeting. Pastor Allen was leading us into the knowledge of Christ, and I was able to call on Jesus, my Lord. This gave me such happiness and joy.

That week, the Lord miraculously provided for us. He paid all our bills and our rent. I wanted to share my new faith with my loved ones. But I knew that my family would be very upset. They already believed that I was a failure and were depressed over my second divorce. Instead, I called one of my Muslim friends and told her what had happened.

She got very upset and said, "You were born as a Muslim, and you will die as a Muslim. Do not let those Christians brainwash you. Okay? Are you choosing to go to hell willingly?"

I hung up the phone heartbroken, with guilt and doubt flooding my thinking. I went to bed in doubt and discouragement. Was she right? Was I just going crazy or being brainwashed? While praying in bed, I said, "Lord Jesus, You know how I feel right now. Please give me a sign that will encourage me to know that I didn't make a mistake in accepting You after all. Please do something."

After I fell asleep, I had a dream. I was in a room with some Christians. They were praising and worshiping the Lord and were speaking in different tongues—just like Norma had done when she prayed over my daughter. Then they all knelt down and lifted up their hands. Just after doing this, the presence of God filled the room. Then an invisible hand started writing on the wall with blood, scribbling the name of Jesus over and over. In my dream, my heart was weak. I woke up in tears.

In that moment, I couldn't open my eyes. I was terrified. The presence of the Lord was still in my bedroom. I knew that Jesus was in the room. I had no doubt. My heart was faint.

Quivering, I said, "My Lord, my heart cannot contain Your presence. Please let me live. If You stay, I will die."

He was so gentle with me. He tenderly acknowledged my prayer, and His presence left my room. Then I was able to open my eyes. As I did, I saw a huge cross made from light in the middle of my room. My bedroom was completely dark, since I had my curtains closed and it was the middle of the night. This beautiful cross had been left by the Lord to minister to me. I said, "Thank You, Lord Jesus, I will never doubt

You again! Thank You for encouraging me, Lord." I stayed awake for the rest of the night, looking at this cross. I did not want to forget this encounter with Jesus.

Since that night, I have been through many tests and trials. But I have never lost hope, and my faith is in Christ's saving and delivering power. Jesus was and still is the God of all miracles.

When I came to Jesus Christ, I denied myself. I gave up my own will for His. My wisdom had failed. I gave up trying to solve every problem or answer every question. When I made the decision to become weak, then the Lord made me strong.

As a new woman, I started seeing the world through the Lord's eyes. I saw how much everybody was trying to survive on their own strength. The New Age movement provided "Believe in Yourself" seminars. Like the communists back in Turkey with their utopian dreams, their approach sounded feasible, but they had no real-life ability to change anything. The New Age movement fell far short of any goals I wanted to attain spiritually. I desired to worship the Creator, my Lord Jesus, who desired to have a personal relationship with me. So I finally gave up all of these false religions that I had once followed. Doing everything my way, I was a failure. But with Jesus, doing everything His way, I was at last victorious.

> *Oh, to be saved from myself dear Lord,*
> *Oh, to be lost in Thee!*
> *Oh, that it might be no more I.*
> *But Christ that lives in me.*
> (A.B. Simpson)

Months later, Millennium Church decided to relocate to a new city.

Soon, I was going to be without a job. But God used Rudy to rescue me. "This company will relocate in couple of months," he told me. "You are very smart. If you are willing, I will give you a lot of materials to study so you can learn to become a bookkeeper." I eagerly agreed, as I could not afford to be without a paycheck for even a week. Rudy trained me as if I was a sponge. Since the Lord was in my life now, I wanted to believe that He would open up many job opportunities for me.

Chapter 34:

Small Beginnings: Ministry

After Jesus Christ saved me that day in Rudy's office, I wanted to serve God with all that I had. I had and have such zeal for Christ. What He has done for me is amazing. Words are not enough to express how His miraculous touch changed my entire being.

That fire in me for Jesus increased each day. I still have that increasing fire. Some Christians have said to me, "In time, you will be more calm and balanced." I answer them, "I don't want to be calm. I don't want to be balanced if it means losing my zeal and fire for Christ." How could you be calm if you were blind your entire life and suddenly your eyes were opened, and you could see the beauty of nature and the color of the sky and the sun? How can you be calm when you are broken in pieces, and then with one touch God makes you whole and you can walk and run and jump?

I want all the world to know what Jesus Christ has done for me. I want them to know so they will know that God can do it for them too.

This fire consumes me. It is inexpressible.

The prophet Jeremiah said,

> *But if I say, "I will not mention him*
> *or speak any more in his name,"*
> *his word is in my heart like a fire,*
> *a fire shut up in my bones.*
> *I am weary of holding it in;*
> *indeed, I cannot* (Jeremiah 20:9).

I just feel the same way. I am weary of holding it in when I am stopped from proclaiming His name.

There was no such thing as a waiting and growing period in my Christian walk. It isn't that way for everyone, but it was for me. I was born again and thrown into the ministry without any advance notice.

Of course, that doesn't mean I was perfect! God was still dealing with my shortcomings. I was humbled to be able to serve Him. One morning, I found myself struggling with my failures right before I was going to speak in front of thousands. I still had bitterness and stubbornness in my heart. I was operating in many ways in flesh rather than Spirit. I was only several months old in the Lord.

That morning, I was under a severe attack. I asked the Lord in tears on my knees, "Lord, look at my heart. I still have so much junk in me. How can You use me like this? I am so imperfect in many ways. I do not deserve You; I do not deserve this ministry."

God whispered gently, "You are right: you do not deserve any of these things. You are right: you are very imperfect. If you wait to be perfect to serve Me, it will never happen. As you acknowledge your sins before Me and have a repentant heart, My Spirit will continually perfect you. But the job will never be complete until the day you are with Me."

I cleaned my face and dried my tears and went up to the pulpit. God's power and anointing was greater than ever before. Those are the times when you know: it is not you doing it, but Him. And it is more humbling than anything else. God's kindness humbled me and still humbles me. It brings brokenness. I have said it many times: "If God can use me, He can use anybody."

The very first time I was asked to share my testimony, I was terrified. First, I didn't know the meaning of "Testimony". I had to look into the dictionary and learned that I was going to speak in front of a crowd. I was only three months old in the Lord. My insecurities got in the way. The devil started throwing his darts at me. Repeatedly, he said, "You are not going to make it. You are going to look like a fool. Nobody will understand your English." I was a baby Christian, and I believed those lies. However, I was already scheduled to give my testimony in a church. I was going to have to do it by faith. I wrote my testimony on paper, modifying it several times. I would read it over and over again to myself, but I was not satisfied with the results. In my mind, Satan was right. I did sound terrible.

When the day came for me to share my testimony, I was shaking like a leaf. I told myself, "At least I can do this for Jesus, especially since He has done so much for me. I want to become a fool for Him, not for the devil."

I walked up to the church pulpit in fear and gave my complete testimony within about twenty minutes. I didn't even know how to quote a verse from the Bible. All I knew was that Jesus had touched me and changed me. I read a passage at the very end of the Bible, since it seemed easy enough for me. It was from the last page of the book of Revelation: "Come, Lord Jesus."

When I finished giving my testimony, I was pleasantly surprised when I looked up and saw many tearful eyes. Many people started to come and filled the altars. Yet the devil said to my mind, "It was a waste of time. Nobody understood you. They cried because they pitied you. You are a clown." Oh, what a terrible liar the devil is! We must know how to shut him up. I walked to an empty seat and sat down. Then the pastor gave a closing challenge which encompassed my testimony and said a closing prayer.

As soon as the service was over, a young woman I had never seen before came up to me. She said, "I have been through the same things." Then she continued, "I woke up this morning planning my suicide. I have two children. I wanted to kill myself because I had no hope for my life. I am a failure. I was planning to drown myself in the river behind this church. But for some reason, I entered this church today. Then I heard you sharing your past pains and struggles. I started having hope for myself too. I said to myself, 'If Jesus did it for this woman, He will do the same thing for me.'" We hugged each other and cried for a while. Then she gave her heart to the Lord and left the church with a new Lord and Savior.

During my first year in ministry, I received an invitation to preach to a large congregation. Just after receiving this invitation, I fell on my knees and cried out to God. I said, "Lord, how can you use me with so much imperfection in my heart? I am so messed up in my thinking." Nevertheless, I prayed, "But for You, Lord Jesus, I will always proclaim Your name wherever I go. As long as I live, I will serve You, Jesus. This is my promise to You."

After this promise, the Lord started to open tremendous doors. I have been preaching since I was three months old in the Lord. There were times I didn't feel worthy to preach from a church pulpit. I failed the Lord many times. Yet, I was conscious of these failures in my heart. I was continuously seeking repentance and reconciliation with the Lord.

Once, I was preaching at a women's conference. God performed many miracles in this service. He revealed to me several prophesies and words of knowledge that I gave at the end of my message. Women from many denominations and nationalities started to fall under the Holy Ghost's power. They were lying on the carpet every which way. I observed this phenomenon with awe.

Right then and there I told the Lord, "Oh, my Lord, who am I that You sent Your Spirit upon Your servant so powerfully and these incredible things happened?" The Lord, in an inner voice, replied back to me, "Işık, you can now realize and appreciate how much I blessed this service with your little obedience to me. Now, imagine if you were even more obedient to Me, how much more power I would pour down on all your services!"

Everyone wants to hear the voice of God. I hear many people saying, "Please pray for me, I need to hear from God," or "I haven't heard from God for so long." But the most important part of our walk with God is not only hearing His voice, but obeying to His voice. And most of the time we fail to do that. We can hear His voice through reading the Bible. The question is, are we obeying? This was a challenge for me. I had to learn to obey even when it hurt to obey.

Chapter 35:

Miracle after Miracle

One night I woke up in the middle of the night with loud banging on my front door. When I got to the door and opened it, I saw three Muslim women begging for help. One of them was very sick. I found out later that they were not financially well off enough to have health insurance and go to the emergency room. The sick woman appeared to be paralyzed from the waist down. The other two women were dragging her into my front room.

I didn't know what they expected from me. I was a new believer in my Christian walk, and I had no clue how they had found me. One of the ladies said, "Please pray for her, she is dying." "Pray?" I exclaimed. *They want me to pray for this sick lady?* I had just woken up. And I didn't even know for sure if she could be healed! I didn't have enough faith.

Very naively I asked, "Pray for what?"

"Pray for her healing," one of the ladies said.

There were three Muslim women in front of me who had more faith than I did in my Savior Jesus Christ's healing power. Without any expectation, just by obedience, I laid my hand on the sick woman. All I was able to say was, "Be healed in the name of Jesus. Amen." This woman, who was in great pain just a few moments ago, was healed instantly. I was in shock. Two of the women surrendered their lives to Jesus at that same time the sick woman was healed.

The next day, I woke up wondering if it had been a dream. Then my phone rang. The caller was the woman who was paralyzed, and she had called to thank me for praying.

God taught me a great lesson that day. It was not my faith or my feeble prayer that healed her. It was the name of Jesus. Just because of my obedience to lay my hand on her and pray in the powerful name of Jesus, she was healed.

I have many Christian friends. Some of them are terribly hesitant to lay hands on a sick person and pray. They say, "What if I pray and the person doesn't get healed?" They must understand if they obey by laying hands on the sick and praying in Jesus's name without doubting, Jesus Christ will bring the miracles.

The Lord may heal a sick person or He may not. That shouldn't be my concern at all. My focus should be on His power and His ability to heal, not on His reasons for not healing. It is not my place to question Him. And it is not about how much faith I have. My responsibility is to obey the Lord by praying over the sick in His name.

It is by obedience, not sacrifice.

Because of that night and the lesson the Lord taught me through it, I now have great compassion for the sick. Whenever I see a person in a wheelchair, or a blind person or someone with any kind of disease, I have a strong urge to lay my hands on that sick person and pray in the name of Jesus. I used to hesitate to do this act of kindness.

Not anymore.

There have been times when I prayed for people and they received healing. There have been other times when they didn't. But I must remember that I do not heal them. Jesus does. Whenever I have the urge to pray for a person, I lay my hands on them and pray in the name of Jesus. And because of my willingness and obedience to the Lord, I have witnessed many miracles.

When people question the Lord's healing after I pray and nothing happens, this is their problem, not mine. I serve a limitless God. If anyone wants to limit the Lord's ability with their disbelief, then that is the result of their minuscule faith.

There was a great woman of God, Kathryn Kulman, who lived before my time and was used by God mightily in a healing ministry. One day, I was searching the Internet for her works, and I came across another article. The person who wrote this article was dedicating his time and effort to try to prove that healings were not real. He went to doctors to get their opinions and advice.

Why would someone do that? I asked myself. *Why do people question God's power instead of praising Him for His greatness? O ye of little faith!* The Pharisees in the New Testament did the same thing. I believe such questioning is a great reproach on God.

After the Lord's miraculous healing of the paralyzed Muslim woman who came to my door, other Muslim women started calling me for their healings as well. The Lord healed them one by one.

One day, I received a phone call from two Muslim women who were sisters. They were living a few hours away from me in another town. They asked me to recommend a church to visit. They were both going through divorces and experiencing depression. One of the women was having a lot of health problems. I prayed and then started to search for a good church in their neighborhood. I found one through my own church. I called them to relate the information to them. They were excited. They even invited me and Melis to go to this church with them.

The next Sunday morning, we all went to that church with their children. There was evidence that the presence of God was in the service. As the choir started to sing, one of the Muslim women started weeping, and then the other one joined in also. The Holy Spirit must have been pricking their hearts.

After the service, one of the women said, "A little voice whispered in my ear and said that this old man in the choir should pray over me." She pointed out that man for us. I said, "Well, we will go and ask him." As we were going toward him, he was coming toward us. When we reached him, I said, "Sir, my friends are Muslims, and one of them heard a little whisper that you should pray over her." He answered, "The Lord told me I was going to her for the same reason."

Before he prayed for her, he remained quiet in a silent prayer. Then he prayed aloud for her lower back to be healed. He didn't touch her. He asked me to put my hand on the area of her back where she hurt. And then he put his hand over my hand, gently, and prayed.

Then he said to the Muslim woman, "Please take a seat and take off your shoes. You also need a healing in your feet. Your feet are causing the problem in your lower spine." I was learning some new things. I had no clue about this woman's health problems. She obeyed the old man in awe and sat down on a chair. Then she took off her shoes. He held her feet and repositioned them so that the heels of her feet were lined up. Now we could see that one of her feet was remarkably shorter than the other one. He held her feet together tightly and started praying. Her short foot started to grow out right in front of our eyes! I had never seen anything like this.

I screamed, "I can't believe this is happening!" They all said, "Shush!" I was about to faint in awe when I saw all of her toes match up together on both feet.

Just after this happened, both of these Muslim women surrendered their lives to Jesus. God loves Muslims just as much as He loves Jews, Hindus, Buddhists, and atheists. God is very generous in providing miracles to Muslims. I believe that he wants more Muslims to surrender to Christ. I have witnessed His miracles many times around hurting Muslims.

On another occasion, a Muslim woman brought her autistic child to my church. She had heard about the miracles of Jesus. Her nine-year-old daughter had never talked. This child was one of the most advanced cases of autism I had ever heard about. She only made weird noises and rocked her body back and forth. This woman brought her daughter to me at the end of the church service. I was able to get my pastor's attention so that he could pray for her.

My pastor came over to us, knowing that I needed help. He asked me to translate for her. He began by saying, "Tell her it is not my prayer that will heal her child, it is not what I will say or how I will pray, but the name of Jesus that will heal this child." I translated this to the child's mother, and she nodded as if she understood. Then we laid our hands on the child, and the pastor prayed. He said, "You will have your miracle by the time the sun rises tomorrow morning."

Early the next morning, my phone rang at 6:30 a.m. It was the mother of the autistic child. She was screaming and crying and laughing at the same time. She said that for the first time since her daughter was born, her daughter had woken up crying and calling for her mother.

We rejoiced over this miracle performed by our Lord Jesus.

As I said before, I have witnessed many of Jesus's miracles among the Muslim people. Through all of these miracles of Jesus, my faith continues to grow tremendously. But the best miracle that I have experienced is watching a lost soul being saved from the clutches of Satan. There is no need to lay hands on a person who is giving his or her heart to Jesus. Again, I think this is the best kind of miracle.

Truly, Jesus is a miracle worker. He has done His biggest miracle in my heart. He cleansed my heart, healed my heart, and changed my heart. And He is still working in my heart through His Holy Spirit even now. He is the best heart surgeon I have ever known. Do you need a new heart today? Do you need a heart transplant? Go to Doctor Jesus. I recommend him. He did the best surgery in my heart, and He can do the same for your heart today. It just takes a moment of simple and genuine prayer: "Come, Lord Jesus, into my heart. Wash me from all my sins. Forgive me for my mistakes and disobedience. Come and make my heart your home."

One more miracle needs to be mentioned in this chapter. After I became a Christian, my mother came from Turkey to visit me in America. She was still grieving over my conversion to Christianity, yet she had missed me terribly after being physically separated from me for many years, and so she came. She even agreed to come to church with me. Even though she did not understand anything said in English, she cried during the entire service. She cried during the worship; she cried at the offering; she even cried at the end of the service. The Holy Spirit was touching her in a major way.

During her visit, one night, we were sitting in my living room in silence. I had already prayed before she came to see me, forgiving her for the verbal abuse that I'd grown up with. I had to forgive her for never showing me any affection. I had to forgive her for always being too depressed to take care of me. As we were sitting in complete silence, the Lord ministered to me very gently. I started looking at my mother and loving her in a way that I had never loved her before, almost as if she was my child and I was her mother. I started to understand her for her pain and to see her through the eyes of Jesus. Compassion swelled in my heart.

Even though I knew my mother hated to be touched, I grabbed her and held on to her very tightly. She tried to escape my arms, but I didn't let her go. I held her so tightly that she could hardly breathe. I held her and held her for what seemed like minutes, struggling—and then my mother started weeping in my arms. She was like a little baby, receiving the love she had never received before in her life. We were both weeping. I kissed her and kissed her and kissed her. I touched her hair, and I hugged her more. She was sobbing. She looked at me and could hardly speak, but she said, "I am sorry. I am sorry. I am sorry. I love you." I said, "I know, Mom, and I love you. You are the best mother in this whole world." And I hugged her.

Since then, God has restored our relationship beyond measure. She started reading the Bible and allowing me to minister to her depression and problems on a biblical basis. Truly, Jesus is a miracle worker.

Chapter 36:

Gas Tank Never Empty

In my first two years with Jesus as the Lord of my life, I had a lot of struggles. I was trying hard to be a "good" Christian, yet I still had so many insecurities and evil thoughts. I was not able to capture my thought patterns, and I was easily distracted. I had many carnalities in the way I dressed and spoke. I could not grasp the meaning of holiness, yet I was very judgmental of others. At the same time, I hated my flesh and how easily it succumbed to Satan's tactics.

I was still longing for a male companion. This time, I wanted Jesus to make this union happen. Yet, I was still deceitful in man's ways. I blamed myself and the church I was attending for my being stuck in carnality. The teaching in my church was not very convicting. Yet, I was not ready for stronger teaching then. Meanwhile, I was tormented by my failures as a Christian, and I wanted to please the Lord so much that I was suffering a great deal.

One night, I received a phone call from a preacher and his wife. They had heard about me through one of my friends and were inviting me and my daughter to their house to spend the weekend. They had two daughters whose ages were close to Melis's age. Even though I didn't know this caller, his voice sounded anointed, and he spoke with authority. I wanted to visit them, but I had almost no money to my name and hardly any gas in my car. Their house was in another town, four hours away from mine. I was embarrassed to tell him my situation, but I told him that I had no money or gas in my car.

He said, "Sister, I know that you will have a hard time believing in what I am about to say since your faith is not strong enough yet. But I want to tell you something. I pray right now in the name of Jesus that you will make it to our house with the gas you now have in your car. If you don't make it to our house, then call me and I will bring extra gas to you. But if you believe that the Lord will sustain you, and you make it to our house with the gas you now have in your car, then I promise you that I will fill your tank and give you money and clothing."

I didn't have the kind of faith to trust in the Lord for a miracle like that—yet. But for some reason, I agreed. Then he prayed over the phone, "I pray in the name of Jesus that my sister's tank will not go empty and that she and her daughter will come to our house safely." At the end of his prayer, I knew that I would make the trip with gas to spare. My faith had increased through his faith.

After driving for two straight hours, I noticed that the needle on my gas gauge had hardly moved. I got excited and started praising the Lord.

Miraculously, I made the trip to his house without running out of gas. I was in awe. Because of this miracle, I had great expectations for my visit to their house.

However, I certainly didn't expect what happened next! As soon as I entered their house, this preacher fell on his face and started praying in a different language. He was "speaking in tongues"—and everything he was saying was in perfect Turkish. He was interceding on my behalf and confessing my intimate sins and struggles with God, all of the things I had been praying to the Lord about earlier. There were other people in the room at the time. They were looking at my face, which had probably turned yellow by then. They knew something was happening, but they didn't understand completely what it was. I was the only one in the room who could understand what he was saying.

Then this man of God looked me in the eye. He pointed his finger at me and said with a loud and firm voice, "Sister, I don't know what I just said, but you seemed to understand it. Take it seriously." Then he repeated himself and said, "Take it seriously. You have a high calling that I cannot describe with words. Take it seriously."

At that moment, I fell prostrate on the floor and wept and wept for a long time. Everybody left me alone on the floor with great reverence while they praised God continuously. Something immediately happened in my deeper being, and I knew at that moment that my walk with Jesus was about to be transformed. I asked this preacher to baptize me with water. So the next day he and his family took me to a lake.

During the entire weekend, we studied the Word of God, praised, and prayed. Food was a secondary priority. All our time was devoted to the Lord. They had developed an all-day-and-night prayer life as a family. They were not choosy about the place or time to pray! They would even stop their car on the highway whenever the Holy Spirit revealed to them to pray for a certain situation. I was not accustomed to this. But I adapted to it very well.

When I returned home from this trip to the preacher's house, I was encouraged, changed, and blessed. I also had many questions in my mind about the church I was attending. I desired a church with deeper teaching. I read in Uncle Arthur's book *Around the World in 88 Years* that, "Once you know the fire, you cannot live on smoke." I started searching for that fire. From that little trip to the preacher's house, I realized that Jesus had lit that kind of fire in me while I was prostrated on the floor praising the Lord. I knew at that moment that nothing else could satisfy me but the fire of God.

Chapter 37:

Don't Cry, Mother

Melis is a grace-giver, and I have learned so much from her. Born during my second marriage, she has been through everything with me.

After my job with Rudy ended, I worked as an assistant in a small company. The job didn't really pay well enough, so I needed extra money. I offered to clean condos. I had to take my daughter with me, since I had no one to take care of her. A very ill, elderly man had just moved out of the first condo I went to clean, and I was warned that the place would be in very bad shape. "I don't mind," I said, "I need to pay my bills." It is hard to describe how despicable that place looked. The ill man had urinated almost everywhere possible. I cleaned a spot on the floor and laid a towel down so my daughter could sit on a clean spot and play with a toy while I cleaned the rest of the condo. She was only five years old at the time.

After maybe five minutes had passed, she came up to me, and said, "I must help."

I said, "No, honey, it is bad for you."

She started crying, "I must help. I must help. Mom, I love you." I gave her extra gloves to wear, and she started to help me with as much strength as she could give.

When I returned the keys to my boss, he gave me a check to pay for my efforts. Then he went to inspect my work. He came back angry.

I said, "What happened?"

He said, "You did not clean inside the oven?"

I said, "It is impossible! Inside of the oven something was burnt; it is all black. I do not know of anything that exists to clean that." He was still angry. I stopped defending myself and handed the check back to him.

Melis and I got back into my car. I was in tears, trying to hide my face so she couldn't see me crying. But she leaned over from the backseat and said, "Don't cry, Mother. Jesus is happy. You did a good job." I just looked at her sweet face in awe and whispered, "Yes, He is happy, honey. Yes, He is."

Shortly after this incident, God gave me favor in business. The Lord has brought me from the deepest and darkest pit to the highest mountaintop. Through His blessing, I eventually became president of a multimillion-dollar company.

Even though I had a prestigious position in the company where I worked, I considered it the biggest honor to preach Christ and His beautiful gospel. No amount of money or worldly riches can compare to what I have experienced with the Lord. A life with Jesus has no price tag on it. It cannot be bought with worldly riches.

Chapter 38:

The Gift of a Companion: My First Marriage under God

Several years after being born again, I started attending a new church. Soon after this, I joined the church choir. The choir was made up of nearly one hundred members, and it was greatly anointed. I was humbled to be part of it. At every church service, I shed tears of appreciation for the Lord while singing with the choir.

Before entering the sanctuary, we would pray and share our testimonies with each other. This was the first time in my Christian walk that I was happy and grateful to be a single adult parent. I didn't even desire to become married. I thought Jesus, along with my daughter and me, made a great family.

Of course, some friends in the church would try to be matchmakers for me anyway. They would try to set up a match with one of their male relatives, whether that person was their son, uncle, or brother. But I was very content as to where I was with the Lord and my relationship with Him.

Then I started reading about great women who were dedicated to Jesus as singles, women such as Mother Teresa, and Madam Guyon.

"Who needs a husband?" I said to myself over and over again.

Nonetheless, there was a man in the choir whom I learned had been an active member in the church for over twelve years. John appeared to be a servant of God, but he was also a very simple man. I would see him bring a cup of water to other members in the choir. He would pick up after other people or distribute music to the choir members. His servanthood was very noticeable.

One day, John was giving a cup of water to an elderly member. At that moment, the Lord spoke to me in an inner voice, saying, "This man is going to be your husband." I was terrified. My heart was troubled. I told the Lord, I was not interested in this man at all. I didn't like him as someone should like a member of the opposite sex. I saw him as a brother in the Lord, and that was all. "Oh no, Lord," I answered. I ignored the Lord's voice on that subject for a long time. John and I never even said hi to each other. After my distressed conversation with the Lord, I continued growing in Him and not focusing on anyone for a personal relationship.

All kinds of friends tried to do me a favor by attempting to match me up, but none of these endeavors materialized since I had already made up my mind to remain single. I had found happiness in Jesus Christ. I found incredible satisfaction in living my life with Him alone. My daughter and I bonded better than ever during this period of time. I was grateful to the Lord for bringing me to this state of not needing someone. It was the first time in my life that I felt free.

My parents couldn't believe I wanted to be alone. Their daughter, the woman they thought they knew, couldn't survive without a relationship with a man! They had to realize that this new freedom was provided for me through a supernatural life with my Lord. I was drinking from the Lord's living water, and I was not thirsty anymore. I was not thirsty for any human relationship, any human mate. I was alone, but not lonely. This was an unseen miracle provided for me by my Savior Jesus. My friends from my former religion would debate with me by throwing all kinds of darts of doubt and condemnation against me about my relationship with Jesus Christ. I was subject to their insults about my new faith in Christ, and I often felt beaten up as a baby in my walk with God. But I remembered this miraculous transformation in my heart and was encouraged.

Many times, we focus on the visible manifestations of God. It is our human nature to seek what we are able to see. Yet, there are greater miracles than raising one from the dead. Transforming a man's heart is a bigger miracle. Taking the heart of a murderer, thief, or adulterer and transforming it into a heart for God is too wonderful to comprehend. The purifying and cleansing power of Jesus Christ cleanses our souls from the stains of sin. This is the bigger miracle.

God did His biggest miracle in my heart by freeing me from my selfishness, immorality, and dependency on man. It was a big relief for me to be set free from these chains of bondage.

Then, unexpectedly, the man whom the Lord had chosen for me (and whom I was still ignoring) tried to phone me. I was in my office at work, praying silently. I didn't answer the phone, but continued praying. My prayer was about God's will in my life. It was Friday, and already a mother from another church was pushing me hard to visit her that night with my daughter in order to meet her son. She was a dear friend of mine and was desperate for her middle-aged son to become married.

I was on my knees, praying in my office and asking for the Lord's will to be done in my life. At the same time, the humble man who brought water to choir members was calling my number. When I finished praying I looked at my phone for the missed call. I didn't recognize the number. Then I listened to the message. John was inviting me and Melis to a baseball game. He said that approximately thirty coworkers were going with him to the same event.

At first, I thought it was very bold of him to call me since I hadn't given him my phone number. Then I thought it was very proper of him to invite me and my daughter together, since this event would be crowded. The invitation really couldn't be called a date. That was a good thing, since I hated the word "date" at this period in my life!

Then I remembered my prayer for God's will to be done. I also recalled what the Lord had revealed to me in the choir: "This man is going to be your husband."

In order to keep myself from being misled about this invitation from John, I started calling my accountability partners within the church. First I called one of my mentors, and then other people I could trust, to find out more about this man. One of these was my associate pastor. They all informed me that John was a man of God, not perfect, of course, yet a true and humble servant. They also respected his idea of taking my daughter and me to this baseball game instead of inviting me only.

Since I had failed so much in relationships in the past and had no confidence in myself, I did one more thing that even amazed me: I ran a criminal background check on the Internet to check him out further. The Lord had already revealed to me that John was the one, but I didn't receive it even from Him. I didn't trust my own judgment. I confirmed with other members of my church, as God's approval was not enough. Then I had to do this one last thing. I thought that if he had a criminal record of domestic violence or child abuse or molestation, my answer would be a big *no*.

But the criminal background check came out clean. I finally returned John's phone call, telling him that my daughter and I would like to go with him to the ballgame. At a later date, when I told the associate pastor and John about my thorough investigation, they broke out in loud laughter.

From the moment we met and went to the baseball game, the Lord's presence was in our midst. John was proper and respectful in every way that a Christian man ought to be. We got to know each other while Melis and other people were around. He used every effort not to place us in situations that would be tempting to both of us. He was also humble enough to admit his past failures and didn't hesitate to share his mistakes.

During this period of acquaintance, we didn't share any romantic moments together. Our relationship was more on a spiritual basis than a romantic one, and it was sweet. In a short period of time, we became best friends. John was a simple man. He never tried to look different to impress me. I liked him for that even more. Even though he was simple, there was such depth and intellect in him. His dedication to the Word of God was amazing. I had met very few people in my Christian walk who had his kind of discipline in studying the Word of God. We served the Lord together on different occasions in church settings, going on ministry outreaches together and being involved in the prison ministry.

He never once asked me to leave Melis with a babysitter. Even when close friends at our church offered to babysit, he didn't feel comfortable about letting them. My daughter began to love him, and she asked about him all the time.

One day she said, "Mom, I love him, and I know that he loves me too. He doesn't love me just to win you. He loves me just for who I am. If you ever get married, I wish that he will be the one."

She was only seven years old.

Melis was visiting her biological father every other weekend. One day John and I were picking up her from her father's house. He was living with a girlfriend. When John met my ex-husband, my ex told us that he'd been having a bad day.

John said, "Can we pray for you?" My former husband smiled and said, "That would be very nice." Then John and I prayed for him.

Later, John and my former husband saw each other many times on different occasions. From these situations, a warm friendship was established between them. Only the Lord can do things like this! At one time, my former husband and I were enemies. Now, God was doing miracles in both our hearts as a divorced couple.

One day, very unexpectedly, my former husband called me on the phone and said, "I never thought I could say this. But I am going to say it anyway. If you ever get married again, I wish John would be that man. He is humble and loving. He is also very good with our daughter. I feel comfortable about him being with her."

Oh boy! How many more confirmations or signs would I ask from God? I did not know. All I knew was that I was not ready to get married.

It was a beautiful summer morning when John asked me to meet him for lunch. After we ate, he gave me a beautiful, large gift wrapped box, and from that big box came a little one. Inside it was a beautiful diamond ring.

Gently, John said, "I have made some wrong choices in my life. A few times I thought I had met the right person, and then she turned out to be carnally minded. These women turned out be very worldly people trying to put on the appearance of spiritual giants. I was disappointed in them as well as in myself. For this reason, I waited for months before approaching you about marriage. I just prayed and stood still. I have never met anyone like you. I love you, but moreover, I love the Lord Jesus in you. I know your calling is to serve God. If you accept me as your husband, I will serve the Lord wholeheartedly by your side."

I took the ring and said, "Yes." I was flattered . . . and yet, I was not ready. I had failed so many times in the same area that I had come to a conclusion: I will never do this right.

After a few days I gave the ring back, asking for more time to pray for God's will. John was heartbroken, yet he was mature and faithful enough to wait upon the Lord. He was forty-seven years old at that time and had been single all his life. He said, "I have waited this long, I am willing to wait longer."

We continued ministering and witnessing to others together. Once we went to a different church at the request of two Muslim women. They were living in another town a few hours from us and wanted us to take them to a local Christian church. The guest speaker for that day was from Africa. This man of God had a heavier accent than mine, yet the anointing upon him was extraordinary. At the end of his message, he gave specific words of knowledge to several individuals as the Lord led him. Throughout the sanctuary, he touched people. Nearly everyone he touched fell out under the power of the Holy Spirit. Nearly everybody was on the floor.

I was standing with my Muslim friends along with Melis and John. This guest speaker came up to me and said, "Sister, you have a high calling from the Lord. But you must be equipped and established." He repeated, "Be equipped and established." I didn't get it right away. His anointed voice echoed in my heart. *"Be equipped and established."*

That following Sunday, we went to our own church. During the service, they announced their school of ministry program. This was an eight-month, intense program for individuals who were being called into full-time ministry. As soon as I heard about the program, the Holy Spirit confirmed in me that this was the way to be equipped and established for my future ministry. I signed up without any hesitation.

When I received the requirements for attending the program, I learned that for participants, being engaged or courting was not allowed. The administrators wanted the attendees' complete attention and devotion toward the ministry. John knew about these requirements already, since he had graduated from the same program several years before.

This program was really a challenging experience for our relationship. We had decided to follow God's will and set our relationship aside while I attended these classes. John displayed a lot of integrity and respect toward God's calling on my life. He was, of course, hoping one day to be linked with me in holy matrimony, serving the Lord mutually. But for eight months, we saw each other only once in a while with a crowd, friends, or in a Bible study class.

This waiting period matured both of us. Our separation helped us to surrender our wills to God's divine will and purpose. We chose to pray and seek the Lord apart from each other.

Months passed, and my graduation ceremony was scheduled. I still had a few days left when one morning I woke up with a release in my mind and heart. I knew the Lord was granting me permission to accept John's proposal. The Lord specifically revealed to me that I was to go and buy a wedding gown for myself. Meanwhile, as John related to me later, he was debating whether to call me by phone since I was still concentrating on my studies before graduation. He wanted to propose to me again.

When my cell phone rang, I was in the bridal shop trying on a wedding gown to surprise him.

He said, "Hello. I am sorry, I didn't mean to bother you. I just thought to call you. How are you?"

I said with joy, "I am great. And you?"

He said, "I am okay, I guess." He paused. "You sound happy. What are you doing?"

I said, "I am buying a wedding gown."

He paused again, thinking it was a bad joke or something like that.

I repeated, "I am trying on a wedding gown . . . if you still want me to wear that engagement ring."

Immediately, I heard him shouting on the phone: "Hallelujah! Oh, thank You, Lord!"

We scheduled our wedding to be performed three months later. Almost immediately, we began to experience some opposition toward our marriage. John was working for a ministry, and it was not a lucrative enough career to support a family. Even my close friends, who seemed to be in complete support, were busy behind our backs with their negative criticisms. This was related to me rudely by some of my friends, who were well-meaning but would tell me that the Lord had told them this and that, all of it discouraging. But I had so much assurance from the Lord, and His peace guided us all the way to the altar to be married.

Man looks at the outward appearance, but the Lord looks at the heart (1 Samuel 16:7).

I can attest to the great depth to which my husband has a humble heart. He does not display any selfish ambition or greed for money. I admire his righteousness. Although he did not promise me a lavish lifestyle, he tithed and gave generously to our church. His example of stewardship had an extraordinary impact on me. The richness I discovered in him made me fall in love with him even more.

When we announced our wedding date, hundreds of people came to us and asked if we needed any help. Some of those people included choir and orchestra members and so on. These were people who knew his and my testimony and rejoiced with us about our union.

We had a glorious wedding. Over three hundred people attended. My only blood relative who could attend the wedding was my mother. My husband does not have a large family either. But we had a huge church family in attendance.

My husband proposed to my daughter on the platform at the wedding with a ring to become her father. Melis took this proposal very seriously. It was beautiful.

Everything was like a fairy tale, and God had ordained it. It was a victorious day against the devil, a day of God's glorious promises coming true. God took me from the deepest and darkest pit and placed me on the highest mountain. I am eternally thankful. The Bible tells us that every good gift comes from above. Our heavenly Father wants to give us even more than we can ever imagine.

My husband received three raises at work after we had been married one year. He was also promoted to a supervisory position. God's timing and His plans are perfect, if we just wait upon the Lord!

"But those who hope in the Lord will renew their strength.

They will soar on wings like eagles; they will run and not grow
weary, they will walk and not be faint," (Isaiah 40:31).

At this point, I want to assure you there is no perfect marriage, as there are no perfect couples. I owe it to you to be honest and not to mislead you. Through the years, as a couple, we went through trials and tribulations. I came with some baggage from my past which came to the surface through very dark ordeals such as losing a child and series of health problems. My husband had his share of baggage too. A few years ago, we lost a pregnancy when it was six months old. We experienced very dark days. We dealt with grief, anger and shame. Now, as we look back, we understand better and even appreciate God for allowing such a trial. We have lost friends during those days - *if you can consider them true friends* - and were condemned and slandered by some. We got a glimpse of what Job went through with his wife and friends. Sometimes Jesus allows you to go through the dark valleys to shake you before placing you on a mountain top. Every suffering, every disappointment and failure can be an opportunity for a glorious beginning if you don't miss the profound teaching behind it.

"The end of the matter is better than its beginning,"
(Ecclesiastes 7:8).

A friend once told me about a young preacher who was on fire for the Lord. Not only was he a servant of God, but he was also single and very handsome. I have never seen him, but as far as I understood, many single women were falling in love with him right and left. Mothers were introducing their daughters to him. But he waited faithfully for years for God's will. Everybody was wondering who the chosen one would be. Then, suddenly, the shocking news of his engagement spread throughout the church. However, the announcement itself was not the most surprising part: the unusual part was that the bride-to-be had no legs. She had been destined to be in a wheelchair all of her life.

Many people in this church were very skeptical. They asked, "How can this be? Is he mad?" One day, this young preacher became very tired of the gossip. While he was preaching from the pulpit on God's unconditional love, he paused and wept. He said he would marry a woman in a heartbeat who had no legs and a heart that was madly in love with Jesus rather than marry a girl who had everything but no love for Christ. He said that when he looked at his fiancée, all he saw was the glowing beauty of the Lord Jesus Christ. He said that she was the most beautiful creature on the face of this earth.

Today, they are happily married with three beautiful children, and all of them are serving the Lord as a family. We can only love as much as the love of God resides in us. God's love is the measure of true love that one person can give to another.

Chapter 39:

Fire Does Not Come to an Empty Altar

Two days before a recent Christmas, I went to see a ninety-six-year-old preacher by the name of "Uncle Arthur", who came from the country of Wales, near England. This man was one of the preachers under the anointing of the Welsh revival who had preached for decades with Smith Wigglesworth. I heard him preach a few years ago, and he impacted my life a great deal.

Even at his age, Uncle Arthur was still preaching in Wales. A man of his age would not be there showing off his spirituality—he was a man of true power. He said with his strong Welsh accent, "Sister, two days before Christmas, everybody is shopping or partying. I do not need to be a prophet to tell you, you are here because you are seeking more, and you have dreams. Are you dreaming revival?" I remained silent, yet my tears started to roll down my cheeks just from hearing the word revival. It had been my dream since the day Jesus lit a fire in me in that preacher's house.

He paused. Then, with a loud voice which sounded like a thunderstorm, he said, "You dream revival, more fire. Now listen: fire does not come to an empty altar." He repeated, "Fire does not come to an empty altar. What brings the fire to the altar? Your ashes do not burn, they are your past. Your gold is your glory to God, and it does not burn. Fire refines the gold, but doesn't burn the gold. Your works do not burn; they are rubbish. Do not focus on how many thousands of people you are preaching to."

This man didn't even know my name. I had showed up, and he had accepted me. He said to me, "If you will preach to millions, still fire may not come. Only wood will burn. The altar needs the wood. What is wood?" He said, "Wood is insignificant. It is wood. It doesn't have a name. It is death. Once it was alive. It was a tree, but now it is death. The question is, will you become that insignificant wood, willing to burn at the altar for the perfect lamb? When you become wood, people will only see the ultimate sacrifice, the perfect lamb. The Father will be well pleased to send the fire, because the perfect lamb's aroma will reach out to heavens and to the nations. But you will be just the wood without a name, willing to burn to bring glory to the Father."

He continued: "Listen, here is the secret. I am almost one hundred years old, and I came all the way here from Wales only for one man. I thought I came for one man. But God made it two with you. But actually, I came for one man. He is coming all the way from Mexico to meet me. He has lost everything. He fell short. He failed. He lost his ministry, his wife, his children, his friends, and his dignity. Everybody left him. I came here to minister to that one man, a nobody, who is an outcast."

He expounded further: "If you want your dreams to come true, cherish the small group in your house with all your heart. Continue to love that one man or woman who is struggling, who is hurting, who is an outcast, and who is unloved. Here is the secret to your dreams: one person. Your ministry is growing, but do not despise that one man. Jesus didn't despise one person. Then, who are we to despise? One woman was bleeding for twelve years; one woman was at the well; one man was by the pool suffering thirty-eight years. One person! Jesus died for that one person. Your church will write a history in this nation. But remember, revivals start in the closets; revivals start in the small groups. Fires come to the wood, insignificant, no-named wood. The name of the *perfect lamb* will be glorified. God will send you the revival you have been dreaming about. You will be the burning wood at the altar."

Chapter 40:

Look Unto Him

I once heard a preacher say from the pulpit, "Do not look to me; look to Him, Jesus. I may disappoint you, but Jesus never will." As a spiritual shepherd, my pastor has always directed his flock to the correct source. That source is Jesus.

One day, I received a call from an elderly lady in my church. She said that her dear friend who goes to my former church was very sick in the hospital. She went on to say that no one had visited her yet. When she said this, I became filled with compassion and said, "I am on my way to visit her. I am leaving home right now."

Then the lady on the other end of the phone said, "When I said 'no one' had visited her, I meant the senior pastor. Many people have visited her. But she is upset that the senior pastor has not come."

I got upset and put my jacket back in the closet. My former church had thousands of people in attendance every week. How can one man be everywhere at the same time? Only Jesus can do this. People should understand that they shouldn't be focusing on a man, but on the Lord Himself instead.

When I witness to Muslims, they sometimes say, "Oh, I know one Christian who does this and that bad thing. He is drinking every day, etc." I tell them, "My friend, as long as you have your focus on men, you will always be disappointed by their imperfections. But if you just look at Jesus who is perfect, you will understand why I follow Him."

Look unto Him—look unto Jesus.

Look unto me, and be ye saved, all the ends of the earth: for I
am God, and there is none else," (Isaiah 45:22, KJV).

You have been reading my story in these pages—but the power of
Jesus to save is not just for me. It is for you and for everyone who will
look to Him.

A young man once said,

> *I sometimes think I could have been in darkness now, if it was not*
> *for the goodness of God in sending a snowstorm one Sunday morn-*
> *ing, when I was going to a place and I could go no further, and*
> *came to a little church. In that church there might be a dozen or*
> *fifteen people. The minister did not come that morning because of*
> *the snow storm. A poor man, a shoemaker, a tailor, or something*
> *like that, went up to preach. The scripture in the Bible that was*
> *preached on was Isaiah 45:22. It says, "Look unto Me, and be ye*
> *saved, all the ends of the earth."*
>
> *There was a glimpse of hope for me in the message. He went*
> *on to say: "My dear friends, this is a very simple scripture. It says,*
> *'Look.' Now, that does not take a deal of effort. It isn't lifting your*
> *foot or your finger. It is just 'look.' Well, a man doesn't need to go*
> *to college to learn to look. He can be the biggest fool, and yet he*
> *can look. A man doesn't need to be worth a million a year to look.*
> *Anyone can look. A child can look. But this is what the scripture*
> *says: 'Look unto Me.' Many of you are looking to yourselves for*
> *your circumstances. There is no use looking there. You'll never find*
> *comfort in yourselves."*

Then this good man followed up his text in this way: "Look unto Me; I am sweating great drops of blood. Look unto Me; I am hanging on the Cross. Look! I am dead and buried. Look unto Me. I rise again. Look unto Me. I am sitting at the Father's right hand. O, look to Me! Look to Me! Then he looked at me as he knew that I was a stranger. Then he said, 'Young man, you look very miserable.' Well, I did; but it was never announced publicly before. He continued: 'And you will always be miserable—miserable in life and miserable in death—if you do not obey my text. But if you obey now, this is the moment, you will be saved.' Then he shouted, 'Look to Jesus Christ!' There and then the cloud was gone, the darkness had rolled away, and at that moment I saw the sun. I could have stood at that moment and sung the most enthusiastically of them all the Precious Blood of Christ.[1]

This testimony belongs to a man of God called Charles Spurgeon, who was called "Prince of Preachers" in his time. Spurgeon truly looked to Jesus that day at age fifteen. He did see Jesus. Today, we too must "look unto" Jesus Christ as our Lord and Savior.

Just look! It is simple.

I love to share the story about a woman in the New Testament who had bled for twelve years. She was considered unclean in her community because of her bleeding. She went to the doctors and in the process spent all of her money. Instead of becoming better, her health grew worse. She was living in shame and guilt because of her illness. Everybody in her town knew that she was bleeding continuously. She was considered an outcast. She was abandoned and unloved.

1 Quoted in Arnold Dallimore, Spurgeon: A New Biography (Chicago: Moody Press, 1984), 18–20.

She was rejected. But just look at how this beautiful story unfolds:

> *And a woman was there who had been subject to bleeding for twelve years. She had suffered a great deal under the care of many doctors and had spent all she had, yet instead of getting better she grew worse. When she heard about Jesus, she came up behind him in the crowd and touched his garment, because she thought, "If I just touch his clothes, I will be healed." Immediately her bleeding stopped and she felt in her body that she was freed from her suffering. Then the woman, knowing what had happened to her came and fell at his feet and, trembling with fear, told him the whole truth. He said to her, "Daughter, your faith has healed you. Go in peace and be freed from your suffering,"* (Mark 5:25–29, 33–34).

"Go in peace and be freed from your suffering." This is why Jesus is considered the master. Jesus set people free. He delivered them from their misery and gave them a simple message: "Go in peace and be freed from your suffering."

In John 8, the story of the adulterous woman that impacted me so much when I first heard it at Bible study, Jesus said, "Go and sin no more" (John 8:11, NLT). There is freedom in those words!

I would like to share another story with you from the New Testament. There was a man paralyzed for decades. He had been left behind. He was suffering and in despair. There was no one to help him, he thought. There was no one who cared. He was stuck in this prison of disability for thirty-eight years.

> *Now there is in Jerusalem near the Sheep Gate a pool, which in Aramaic is called Bethesda and which is surrounded by five cov-*

ered colonnades. Here a great number of disabled people used to lie—the blind, the lame, the paralyzed. One who was there had been an invalid for thirty-eight years. When Jesus saw him lying there and learned that he had been in this condition for a long time, he asked him, "Do you want to get well?"

"Sir," the invalid replied, "I have no one to help me into the pool when the water is stirred. While I am trying to get in, someone else goes down ahead of me."

Then Jesus said to him, "Get up! Pick up your mat and walk." At once the man was cured; he picked up his mat and walked (John 5:2–9).

We are all crippled, we are all blind, we are all handicapped so that we can use the hand of God. We can be healed for His glory.

This man by the pool stayed there, paralyzed, for thirty-eight years. He could hardly move. He was crawling on the ground with no progress, no ability to enter the pool. He was bogged down in his circumstances. He was hopeless. When the water was stirred, he would try to get in, but someone else would reach the pool before he did. He was accustomed to being the last one in the pool; for years, no one seemed to care for him. He was a paralyzed man whom no one pitied.

We have all felt this way at some time, haven't we? This would include feeling abandoned. Nobody cares for you. Everybody is ahead of you, and you are the last one. Everybody has got it all together except you.

Well, I have been there too. From my previous experience as a cast-off, I know how he felt. I was hopeless and stranded in my cursed destiny for twenty-eight years. I was in depression for over twenty years. When I observed other people, it felt like everybody was ahead of me. Everybody looked like they had it all put together. I was raised in a dysfunctional Muslim home where there was much verbal abuse between my parents. They would curse each other, slam doors, and break things. My parents belittled me as a child. I lived in shame and guilt. As an adult, I suffered through abusive relationships and my own bad decisions.

But the good news is that God doesn't leave any job unfinished. God doesn't do a halfway job. God's works are complete masterpieces. No one will ever read anything in the Bible stating that the man was in the pool and suffered for another thirty-eight years, or that the woman continued bleeding for the rest of her life.

What you will read in the Bible is that they were healed.

Once Jesus intervenes in our lives, we are healed. These victories start at the point of Jesus' healing power. This healing power of Jesus comes after the sickness, failure, misery, and brokenness of people. When we are about to lose hope and believe the lies of the devil, Jesus comes to rescue us. When we are about to lose faith and accept the condition of being paralyzed and stranded in our prisons, the Lord shows up. Jesus says in the New Testament, "I care for you. You are not abandoned or forsaken anymore. I died for your sins."

Will you believe Him today?

Chapter 41:

To See God

Yet to all who did receive him, to those who believed in his name, he gave the right to become children of God—children born not of natural descent, nor of human decision or a husband's will, but born of God (John 1:12–13).

God, the Creator of the earth and the heavens, supernaturally used His prophets to speak to His creation. No one can see God directly because of God's magnificent power. Moses wanted to see God, so God told him to wait for Him to pass by. He said, "Whoever sees Me will die." This is not because God will punish anyone for seeing Him, but because of His uncontainable existence.

But God was not happy with this distance from us. In order to allow us to see Him, God sent His only Son, Jesus Christ, to earth in human flesh to dwell among us. He ate and talked with men; He healed the sick, gave sight to the blind, and raised the dead. Jesus taught His ways to His people. He loved them very dearly and showed them the way which would lead to eternal life with Him. Then Jesus went to the cross and died on our behalf. Without Him paying the penalty for our sins, we would go to hell. While dying on the cross, Jesus told us by His actions that He loved us. He said that He loved us so much He would die on our behalf. He would sacrifice His life for ours.

Then on the third day, Jesus was resurrected from the dead, so whosoever believes in Him shall also be resurrected with Him. Jesus gave us victory over death. Accepting Jesus as our Lord and Savior changes our eternal destiny: we are destined for heaven instead of hell.

Our old self, that is, our sinful self, died with Christ when He died on the cross for us. We crucify the "old man," ourselves, on this cross just by accepting Him into our hearts. Then He becomes Lord and Savior for us. He saved us from death and hell by resurrecting us with Him. Then we shall live with Him, and Jesus will live in us.

For God so loved the world that he gave His one and only Son,
that whoever believes in Him shall not perish but have eternal
life. For God did not send his Son into the world to condemn
the world but to save the world through Him
(John 3:16–17).

Through Jesus Christ, God becomes our friend. We can be called friends of God by accepting Jesus as our Lord and Savior. And Jesus is a *good* friend. A good friend lays down his life for His friends. Because God, who created the heavens and earth and everything in it, has abundant grace, we can be saved.

Other religions will tell you to do this and do that to achieve acceptance from God. But by dying on the cross for us, Jesus is telling us that "it is finished." Just come to Him and accept Him into your heart. It is a simple step of faith. It only involves a decision. It only requires our free will in giving our hearts to Jesus Christ. When we do, we can be in right standing with the God of the universe. We can be recognized and called sons or daughters by God. Jesus can heal our broken hearts. He can heal our diseases. He can give each of us a new life and a new heart.

If you believe, you are saved from the eternal fire of hell and become a child of God. You are "born again."

After we experience this new birth, we need to pray to Jesus so He can show His will for our lives, and we need to read the Word of God daily. When you read the Word, the Lord will speak to us through His words. It's also important to join a church which lifts up the name of Jesus and practices biblical truths. We should pray that God will bless us richly. Then, we will walk in obedience to God for the rest of our lives. We will serve Him humbly and keep His teachings in our hearts. We will walk in the Spirit by faith, not by sight. In Jesus' name we pray, amen.

Chapter 42:

The Lord Gives Free Will

There is a time for everything,
and a season for every activity under heaven:
a time to be born and a time to die,
a time to plant and a time to uproot,
a time to kill and a time to heal,
a time to tear down and a time to build,
a time to weep and a time to laugh,
a time to mourn and a time to dance,
a time to tear and a time to mend,
a time to be silent and a time to speak,
a time to love and a time to hate,
a time for war and a time for peace
(Ecclesiastes 3:1–4, 7–8).

I say, this is the time to love God and hate evil.

This is the time to speak and not to be silent.

This is the time to fight against tyranny.

This is the time to be obedient as God's servants.

Whatever direction God is leading you, follow Him.

Be with Him in strength and power.

Be with Him in assurance and determination.

Be with Him.

I believe God gives us many chances in our lives to take us from where we are to where He wants us to be. Of course, he gives us free will in getting to our final destiny, whether it be our natural final destiny or the one He has designed for us. Free will brings us back to the One who created us, to reconcile us to Him. That free will can also remove us from His protective hand. Free will can turn this world upside down. That free will can also put us in our own inner prisons, or even in a physical one.

Some of the details mentioned in my story may not be pleasant to read. I share them with you so you can realize that everyone has a free will that will shape his or her life.

This is the time to live for Christ.

When man speaks, it will be forgotten, erased from the minds of those who hear, but when God speaks, it will be written in people's hearts. May God speak to you clearly to advance you to a specific destination that will make your life worth living.

Life without Christ's love is worthless.

Remember, God is love.

From Genesis to Revelation, it is His desire to pour out His everlasting love into our hearts.

It is His desire to show His unconditional love in any and every way that we could possibly imagine.

He is longing to dwell in our hearts.

That is a kind of love that makes this life on earth worth living. His love is unconditional.

> *Your love, O LORD, reaches to the heavens, your faithfulness*
> *to the skies. How priceless is your unfailing love! Both high*
> *and low among men find refuge in the shadow of your wings*
> (Psalm 36:5, 7).

Surely it was for my benefit that I suffered such anguish. In
your love you kept me from the pit of destruction; you have put
all my sins behind your back (Isaiah 38:17).

"Though the mountains be shaken and the hills be removed,
yet my unfailing love for you will not be shaken nor my
covenant of peace be removed," says the Lord, who has
compassion on you (Isaiah 54:10).

My prayer is that we will all experience His love and fall madly in love with Him.

Life will be worth living if we are in love with Christ.

May you have power, together with all the saints, to grasp how
wide and long and high and deep is the love of Christ, and
to know this love that surpasses knowledge—that you may be
filled to the measure of all the fullness of God
(Ephesians 3:18–19).

What is that unconditional love that makes life worth living?

Let's fall madly in love with Jesus. He never fails us, never forsakes us or abandons us. He is always faithful.

IF YOU HAVE FEAR TODAY, "IT IS FINISHED."
IF YOU HAVE SICKNESS, "IT IS FINISHED."
IF YOU HAVE HEARTACHE, "IT IS FINISHED."
IF YOU HAVE GUILT, "IT IS FINISHED."
IF YOU HAVE SHAME, "IT IS FINISHED"
IF YOU HAVE UNFORGIVENESS, "IT IS FINISHED."
IF YOU HAVE HATE, "IT IS FINISHED."
IF YOU HAVE SELF-PITY, "IT IS FINISHED."

*You turned my wailing into dancing; You removed my
sackcloth and clothed me with joy, that my heart may sing to
You and not be silent* (Psalm 30:11–12).

A life worth living is a life with power and authority through Jesus.
David says, "That my heart may sing to You and not be silent."

*But will God really dwell on earth with men? The heavens,
even the highest heavens, cannot contain you. How much less
this temple I have built!* (2 Chronicles 6:18).

My friends, my journey with Christ continues. I pray that you will
begin yours today. Allow Jesus to make your life a masterpiece.

*"For I know the plans I have for you," declares the Lord, "plans
to prosper you and not to harm you, plans to give you hope
and a future. Then you will call upon me and come and pray
to me, and I will listen to you. You will seek me and find me
when you seek me with all your heart. I will be found by you,"
declares the Lord* (Jeremiah 29:11–14).